416

Keep The
Fire Glo

By Pat

Keep t
Rekind

By Pat

The Gi
The Po

Also by

We Ow
Nothing

Keep The Fire Glowing

Pat and Jill Williams
with Jerry Jenkins

Fleming H. Revell Company
Old Tappan, New Jersey

Scripture quotations identified NAS are from the New American Standard Bible, © The Lockman Foundation 1960, 1962, 1963, 1968, 1971, 1973, 1975, 1977.

Scripture quotations identified NIV are taken from the Holy Bible: New International Version. Copyright © 1973, 1978 by the International Bible Society. Used by permission of Zondervan Bible Publishers.

"Who Loves Me," by Laura C. Patterson, reprinted by permission of *Woman's Day* Magazine. Copyright © 1983 by CBS Publications, the Consumer Publishing Division of CBS, Inc.

Excerpts from THE MYSTERY OF MARRIAGE by Mike Mason, copyright © 1985 by Multnomah Press, Portland, Oregon 97266. Used by permission.

Material from LOVE LIFE FOR EVERY MARRIED COUPLE by Ed Wheat, M.D., Copyright © 1980 by Ed Wheat, M.D. Used by permission of The Zondervan Corporation.

Excerpts from FOR THOSE IN LOVE by Lionel Whiston. Copyright © 1983 by Abingdon Press. Used by permission.

Excerpts from HIDE OR SEEK by Dr. James Dobson, copyright © 1974, 1979 by Fleming H. Revell Company.

Excerpt from the article "Will Your Marriage Survive Your Children?" by Marilyn McGinnis. Copyright © 1984 Family Life Today, Pasadena, CA. Reprinted by permission.

Excerpts from "Thoughts on a Son's 13th Birthday," by David C. Fisher. Copyright © 1983 Family Life Today, Pasadena, CA. Reprinted by permission.

Excerpts from "Rabbinical Discipleship at Home," by H. Dennis Fisher, *Moody Monthly,* copyright © 1984. Used by permission.

ISBN 0-8007-1498-9

Copyright © 1986 by Patrick L. M. Williams
and Jill M. P. Williams and Jerry B. Jenkins
Published by Fleming H. Revell Company
Old Tappan, New Jersey 07675
All rights reserved
Printed in the United States of America

TO Dr. James Dobson and Dr. Ed Wheat,
who have had more influence on us and thousands of others
in the areas of child rearing and marriage
than anyone else ever

Contents

Introduction

The Next Exciting Step ...
by Jill Williams

Stunned . . . There's no other word for it.

Hundreds and hundreds and hundreds of letters poured in to our home following the release of *Rekindled* in early 1985. It was a simple narrative, the story of our ten-year marriage, its near collapse, and its miraculous new start.

From a Christian leader:

> I read the book last week in one sitting on a flight. I discovered it was a mistake to read it in public. It was impossible to hold back the tears, especially as I got toward the end of the book. I was embarrassed as I sat on the plane mopping my face.
>
> I want to thank you for being so honest in writing a book like this. It is desperately needed in this day of shattered home life. Just this morning on my desk was a letter from a longtime dear friend announcing in sadness his divorce proceedings. I plan to send him your book immediately, but I am not sure whether or not it may be too late for him.

A sales manager:

> I felt that someone had written my autobiography and used another name. I stopped counting the similarities. Having read your book will forever change my attitudes.

A political figure:

I have let myself get pretty much in the same situation. I'm going to change things at home, just like you did.

A wife:

I thought no one in the world—except the Lord—knew how neglected and unimportant and second-place I felt. Our marriage has been downhill since my husband began coaching— he's so wrapped up in it.

I've just about given up hope. The marriage is not right. Please pray for us. I want more than life itself to have a happy marriage with the one who adored me when we married almost ten years ago.

A pastor:

I personally identified with Pat and saw so much of my wife in Jill. We had a similar D-Day confrontation just two short years ago, which by the grace of God transformed our marriage as well. My ministry goals had left my wife out in the cold.

A wife:

I've been at the place Jill was on her D Day several times. If it wasn't for a few close friends who prayed faithfully for me, I would have cracked up. My husband called it "Feeling sorry for yourself day." He can't understand what I've been trying to tell him for years.

He never helped with the children when they were babies. He has never really shared in the home life at all. I help with the kids' homework and have to take them everywhere, do or supervise all the housework, etc.

I really need his emotional support. When I ask for help, he retorts, "When are you going in to work for me?"

He has a good job and I don't need to work, but he's very materialistic and feels that if I worked we could buy more things.

When I had physical problems after the birth of our second child, he even resented friends coming over to help me out. He felt I was just trying to get out of my work. It's hard to get the kids to help around the house when they see their dad sitting around watching TV or napping.

Our teenage daughter is an honor student but afraid to date because of the type of marriage she sees in her own home.

I remember my husband telling me he loved me years ago, but he won't anymore. When I ask him to PLEASE tell me, he says, "You know I do. I wouldn't put up with you if I didn't."

He thinks a wife is a slave to her husband and that to submit means I'm beneath him. How can I quit when I know what it would do to the children? I guess I'm just tired. Tired of being the strongest. I need someone to lean on.

We knew what God had done for us, He could do for others. And we knew from our reading that not only was divorce becoming epidemic, but even in marriages still intact there was a lack of fire, lack of commitment, lack of love ... even in Christian homes.

We had known from the minute we began telling friends and associates our story that it was one that needed a wider telling. Pastor and radio preacher Charles Swindoll, one of our favorite authors, encouraged us, "You've got to write a book. This story must be told." He suggested the title *Rekindled.* "And let me advise one more thing. Tell it all. Don't hold anything back."

It wasn't easy, but we followed his advice. We worried that people might not be able to identify with us and we might be seen as "fast track" people because Pat is a professional sports executive and speaker and I am a vocalist and violinist as well as a mother.

But the point was: Our problems were typical, more typical even than we knew. The trouble in our marriage was not infidelity, it was fidelity with fatigue, a marriage gone soft and sour due to lack of attention. It was lack of communication that nearly killed us.

Pat was hard driving, successful, at the top of his career. He was general manager of the Philadelphia 76ers, who would in

1983 become the world champions. He spoke, he memorized Scripture, he studied his Bible an hour a day, he kept up with other pro teams and college prospects by traveling or watching games on cable TV. All his time was taken up with valuable, important things—but his priorities were wrong. He had left his *wife* out of his *life*.

He jogged, he ate health food. He was everything a woman is supposed to want in a husband. Except, I didn't want everything. I just wanted him. His time. His attention. Emotionally, I was dying and he didn't even know it.

When I occasionally got his attention, Pat would patch things up with dinner out or a gift of flowers. But finally, after ten years, D Day arrived. I had had enough. I got through to him, convinced him he had lost me. I wouldn't leave him, I wouldn't divorce him. Wouldn't do that to him or the children. But I was gone—because love was gone.

Finally, he was convinced. But it was nearly too late. It took a true work of God in Pat's life to wake him up to the problem and lead him to the book, Dr. Ed Wheat's *Love Life for Every Married Couple* (Zondervan, 1980), that eventually saved our marriage.

Rekindled tells the painful story of our rescued marriage and the agonizing process that led to victory. First Pat and eventually I put into practice a simple formula designed by Dr. Wheat. It was called B-E-S-T, an acronym for Blessing, Edifying, Sharing, and Touching, which became the touchstone of our relationship through Christ.

We had been wary at first of basing our book on some of Dr. Ed Wheat's material, but he was so happy with our success and moved by our story that he wept when he read the manuscript and agreed to write the foreword.

The book was given a boost when we were interviewed by Dr. James Dobson on his "Focus on the Family" radio program, and he made thousands of copies available to listeners. Eventually *Moody Monthly* magazine featured excerpts in three consecutive issues.

Rekindled quickly became a best-seller, and not surprisingly, Dr. Wheat's *Love Life* reappeared on the best-seller lists too. The hurt and need we felt was felt by thousands.

Besides dealing with our rescued marriage, *Rekindled* chronicled the growth of our family. We had Jim, Bobby, and Karyn, then adopted two Korean orphans, Andrea and Sarah. Not long after, we added another of our own, Michael.

Some of our friends thought that six children would be too much pressure in the home of a couple whose marriage had nearly ended. But we were committed to each other and to Christ, and for us, it worked. It worked so well that sometimes we think of adopting a couple more! And we always remind people that having children will not save a bad marriage, but they will enlarge the circle of love in a good marriage. *In fact, that is what this book is all about—enlarging the circle of love within a family that has as its center a loving, caring, Christ-committed husband and wife.* Our purpose in writing is to show you how to build the B-E-S-T family possible.

We want to show our readers how to take the next exciting step and to rekindle their family life. No family can survive unless there is a loving marriage. But no marriage can grow unless husband and wife are able to create a family rooted in Christian love and discipline.

Keep the Fire Glowing will show you how to make your family a 1 Corinthians 13 family. It will help you put into practice the rules of love so that you will grow and your children will grow in the fear and admonition of the Lord.

Nothing is more exciting. There is no greater responsibility than to lead your loved ones to Christ. That is the only way to truly *Keep the Fire Glowing.*

... Happy Marriages Build Happy Families   by Pat Williams

There are those who wondered, or at least whose questions made it appear they were wondering, how the B-E-S-T principles we learned from Dr. Wheat were affecting not just our marriage, but our whole family, all six kids.

It's a valid question. It's possible for a couple to become so engrossed in their marital problems that the children are left out in the cold. Too often, the opposite is the case. A troubled marriage causes so much friction that the kids are swept into it, pitted against each parent, and wondering where they really fit in.

Our contention has been that the clichés are right. The best thing a father can do for his children is to love their mother. Happy marriages build happy families.

If a marriage has the characteristics of 1 Corinthians 13: patience, kindness, courtesy, unselfishness, generosity, good temper, guilelessness, sincerity, and humility, there will be security for everyone in the home. And the best way to achieve that is through the B-E-S-T system—by Blessing, Edifying, Sharing, and Touching.

That's certainly true in our case. No more shouting matches. No more silent treatments. Maybe some grouchiness or insensitivity once in a while, but a sense of forgiveness and reconciliation overrides it all.

How does B-E-S-T affect the children? Wonderfully. And how is it still working in our marriage? So well that the sequel to *Rekindled* could not be *Rekindled II.* It seemed logical to some to come back a few years after the D-Day confrontation and all the struggles we endured and find out how the finally happily married couple is doing after the novelty has worn off.

Might have made a good story, especially if we included anecdotes of lapses, of slipping back into old patterns. And wouldn't it have been interesting and dramatic to show that adding two adopted children and another of our own had proved to be a big mistake?

Fortunately for us, B-E-S-T has stood the test. It stood the test when we doubled our child population in the house. It stood the test of my ever-increasing pressure at work and in my ministry. It stood the test of Jill's inbred need for my time and attention.

Nobody's perfect. We still have disagreements of course. Arguments. But the air is cleared quickly because the partner who's strongest at the moment will break the tension with humor, or a gentle reminder, or a touch, or a loving comment.

We're convinced B-E-S-T works for child rearing as well. Maybe that's not what our good friend Dr. Ed Wheat intended for his B-E-S-T principles, but they're so good, they apply to *any* relationship if adapted appropriately.

Blessing

There are four specific ways to bless your family:

1. *To speak well of each person and respond with good words in every situation.* In our marriage, I had failed to praise Jill to others. This bothered Jill and yet I just couldn't bring myself to do it. (*She* was always telling people I was the best speaker she'd ever heard!) Maybe I thought it would sound like bragging—whatever the reason, I had to make a change and start to compliment Jill in public as well as privately.

Speaking well of your spouse or your child means praising him to others—and treading that fine line between praising and bragging. Ever notice that kids bless their parents by speaking well of them naturally? Until they're beaten down with criticism or neglect, children believe mom and dad are the best on the block. The best cook. The best looking. The strongest. The best ballplayer.

It's crucial to praise a child to your mate, in front of the child. "Honey, you should have seen how Jim and Bob stuck up for their sisters today." Or, "You would have been proud of Karyn when she did her chores this morning without being reminded."

Related to speaking well of a child to others is, of course, blessing him by speaking kind words to him. This is a tough one, because often children can be testy and the situation uncomfortable, just as in a marriage relationship.

Regardless, the responsibility of the parent attempting to apply B-E-S-T principles not just to the marriage but also to the family is to respond kindly, no matter how difficult the child is at the moment.

In *Rekindled,* I recommended a ninety-day test that is to be applied to one's mate, children, and anyone else who needs to be on the receiving end of these principles. "You must go ninety straight days, during which you respond with kind, uplifting, encouraging words to everything that comes your way, good or bad. If you blow it, you start over at day one and shoot for ninety again."

2. *To do kind things.* It's no more than the golden rule. We want to remind ourselves of this constantly by asking, "What can I do now that will be a kind act for_____?" Most exciting is when you see the children treating each other this way too.

In our marriage, I decided on freshly squeezed orange juice for Jill every morning. For the children, it might be something different, something especially for each one. Example: A bedtime story for one; pitching the baseball every evening with another. And what we do for ours might be meaningless for yours. If you think children in the same family differ from one another, imagine the differences between children of different families!

One thing is constant, however. Regardless what the kind gesture is that warms up your child, all children are warmed by kindness from mom or dad. Or sister or brother.

3. *To express thankfulness and appreciation verbally.* The key here, of course, is to take the time to notice what each family

member has done that is worthy of a genuine compliment. As we'll discuss in detail in chapter five, kids see through phony praise. But they live and die for the real thing.

4. *To pray for his good and the highest blessing of God in each family member's life.* I use a note on my phone to remind me to pray for Jill. Pictures of our children set at strategic places in the home or office can remind us to pray for them frequently.

I made it a point to treat Jill as a guest in our home. Who gets better treatment than a guest? Imagine the value of treating children that way. Would we nag a guest, holler at him, remind him to clean up his plate?

It's our job to, as Dr. Wheat put it, set the thermostat. That means establishing a climate that allows children to live to their fullest potential.

Edifying

This simply means to support or build up, and it's done by praising. Frequently. Kids eat it up. So do I! So do all of us. I finally came to realize that Jill had little confidence in herself, despite her beauty and her gifts. I hadn't helped matters by my criticizing and needling. Now I try to encourage her and build her up. I have had to learn that teasing can become a habit and can go too far. I hadn't known when to stop.

Peace and harmony in the home are also crucial to the edification of children. Peace and harmony come from really knowing your spouse and children. And you can know them only by taking the time to talk to them and to listen. More on this in later chapters.

Sharing

Dr. Wheat's challenge to me was to share my time, activity, interests, concerns, innermost thoughts, spiritual walk, family objectives, and career goals with Jill. Jill had once said to me, "You think the whole NBA would disintegrate without you." In a way I did. I always had my hand on the throttle and never took a break. I didn't know how to enjoy my family. If we went away for the weekend, I spent half the day on the phone and tried to get back early. Now, I make time for my family, and I wouldn't have it any other way.

Sharing with children, obviously, has to be tailored to their ages. But there's no light like the light that brightens a child's face when he knows he has been included in plans, goals, and objectives. He's made to feel important and loved.

Touching

Dr. Wheat makes touching paramount in marriage, emphasizing that all else is for naught without heavy doses of nonsexual physical contact: "At birth, touch was our first line of communication. The cuddling and loving we received was necessary for our physical well-being. Now that we are adults, very little has changed. We still have a deep need for the warmth, reassurance, and intimacy of nonsexual touching whether we are conscious of it or not." Hugging, holding hands, sitting close together while reading or watching TV can bring warm and wonderful feelings of comfort and support. Dr. Wheat believes that American society is so sex conscious because people are really looking for the intimacy that has been lost through the nonacceptance of touching relationships.

A tender touch tells your child that he's cared for. As it does for a spouse, it calms a child's fears, soothes his pain, brings him comfort, gives him emotional security. Touching doesn't guarantee a happy marriage and happy children, but without it your family life will be lacking an essential and rewarding dimension.

Clearly, the B-E-S-T principles apply to child rearing just as much as to a marriage. With that in mind, and seeing the evident benefits in our own family, we began reading. It isn't as if we hadn't already been voracious readers. The TV in our house is jealous of our thousands of books. We have so many we had to have a librarian come in and catalog them with a reference system and all.

But now we had a mission. If we were going to try to do a book on how a happy marriage can build a happy family, we wanted more than our own limited experience. In the ensuing months between the time this book was conceived and the time it was hatched, it's fair to say that we have read every book and article on the subject written over the last several years.

You'll find help from myriad sources and experts. And here and there we'll drop in Glow Words, some pithy quote that will brightly capture what we've learned, or give you the inspirational spark to brighten your own family life with specific action. Glow words will help illuminate the points we are making in a chapter, and, we trust, set off a spark in your heart for reflection and action.

Because a happy marriage is paramount, we start there. Then we move on to priorities, followed by taking a couple's spiritual base and applying it to the whole family. You'll find that communication is high on our list, and that affirmation comes before discipline.

But there are things to avoid, too. And one is guilt. Too often, parents drive themselves too hard. They set standards so high, they read and study and listen to so much advice that there is no way they can live up to their own ideal of parenthood. Then their children can't live up to the standards either.

Then the guilt sets in. What have we done wrong? But, as Dr. S. Bruce Narramore reminds parents, nowhere in the Bible are we commanded to feel guilty. We do not have to blame ourselves for the wrong decisions our children make. They are individuals with the same freedom of choice that we have. And like us, they are responsible to God for their own actions.

All we can do, with the help of God, is the best we can. Are we pulling back from the advice in this book? No, we're simply saying: We're not perfect parents. We never will be. Neither will you. You must take from this what will help you most, leave the rest, and get on with your job.

One thing that God will give you plenty of is love for your

children. Pray for that special brand of unconditional love that only He can provide. That will cover a multitude of parental shortcomings. Our prayer is that you will enjoy your children and be blessed by a family that is God's B-E-S-T—a true expression of 1 Corinthians 13.

Chapter One

Marriage: The Foundation

> The most important relationship in the family is the marital relationship. It takes primacy over all others, including the parent-child relationship. Both the quality of the parent-child bond and the child's security are largely dependent on the quality of the marital bond.
> Dr. Ross Campbell, *How to Really Love Your Child*

How many times have you heard people say, "These kids are tearing our marriage apart." The fact is, most often the opposite is true. Troubled marriages produce troubled kids. Only very rarely will you hear of happy, harmonious children who are the product of a stormy marriage. Happy kids are the result of a 1 Corinthians 13 marriage.

Children may grow up and distance themselves from a bad situation, even carving out happy marriages and families for themselves, but it will be in spite of, certainly not because of, the way they were raised.

Research shows that divorce begets divorce, abuse begets abuse, alcoholism begets alcoholism, and on and on. Those who use their parents as models will perpetuate more of the same. (One of our children's school friends, however, who is the product of a broken home, has only one major goal in her life—*not* to become like her mother!)

Most people, even those whose marriages are nearly dead,

realize that a broken home is not good for children. That's why so many stay together "a few more years—for the children."

While this is not a humorous subject, we did hear a funny story about this aspect of divorce. A couple in their nineties had been married nearly seventy-five years. The divorce lawyer asked why they were going to let one little spat ruin a lifetime of wedded bliss.

"It's been seven and a half decades of misery," the wife reported.

"Then why did you wait so long?"

"Well, we wanted to wait until the kids were dead."

Are you just hanging on for the sake of your children? You can do better than that. God can turn your marriage around so that your kids not only have a mom and a dad in the house for male and female role models, but also a home with the warmth and security of parents who truly love each other.

True love is not that helpless feeling of romance that makes us think about our beloved every minute. (Billy Graham talks about having to give up his first love when he became a Christian. "It was only puppy love," he admits, "but it was real to the puppy.") True love is an act of the will. Love is as love does, even after we've discovered that our spouse is not perfect. When the puppy love feeling is gone, true love is still there, doing its thing.

Even though the idea of love as an act of the will and not an emotion is now a popular and valid truism, there remain many misconceptions about marital love. In the prologue of Mike Mason's *The Mystery of Marriage* (Multnomah, 1985), he talks about his discovery of what he calls "one of the chief characteristics of love":

> It asks for everything. Not just for a little bit or a whole lot, but for everything. And unless one is challenged to give everything, one is not really in love. But how hard it is to give everything! Indeed, it is impossible. One can make a symbolic gesture of giving all, accompanied by a grand dramatic public statement to that effect (which is what happens at the wedding

ceremony). But that is just a start. The wedding is merely the beginning of a lifelong process of handing over absolutely everything, and not simply everything that one owns but everything that one is.

In *Rekindled* we make it clear that this was one aspect of marriage that neither of us knew. I have to take the lion's share of the heat for treating the wedding—and, indeed, the marriage itself—as an incidental in my life. But Jill, too, while she expected me to change overnight from a sports exec to a devoted husband, hadn't really given up and handed over everything in her life either.

It doesn't work that quickly. First, a couple has to realize what is required. Then the painful process of growing together begins. It can be exciting and dramatic, but it's work, and it's an unnatural sort of growth because we are all intrinsically self-absorbed. But this is a spiritual growth that breaks selfishness for mutuality. Mike Mason continues:

> There is no one who is not broken by this process. It is excruciating and inexorable, and no one can stand up to it. Everyone gets broken, at least a little, on the wheel of love, and the breaking that takes place is like nothing else under the sun.
>
> It is not like the breaking that happens in bankruptcy or in a crop failure or in the loss of a job or the collapse of a lifetime's work. It is not even like the breaking that takes place in a body wracked by a painful disease. For in marriage, the breaking is done by the very heel of love itself.
>
> It is not physical pain or natural disaster or the terrible evil world "out there" that is to blame, but rather it is love, love itself that breaks us. And that is the hardest thing of all to take. For in the wrestling ring of this life, it is love that is our solar plexus. That is where things really hurt. . . .
>
> In the relationship of marriage, it is this very quality of vulnerability that is exposed, exalted, exploited. And this is the thing that can prove to be too much for people, too much to

handle. Many give up and run away, their entire lives collaps-
ing in ruins. But even those who hang on face inevitable ruin,
for they must be broken too.

That conclusion may sound strange, and it is perhaps unfair
to quote this much of author Mason without allowing him to
finish his own point. Briefly, he was saying that a marriage, a
love, need not be ruined by those who stay together and work
at it, but that each person's ego must necessarily suffer and die
for the sake of love.

There is a quote attributed to Théophile Gautier that goes
like this: "To renounce your individuality completely, to see
with another's eyes, to hear with another's ears, to be two and
yet but one, to so melt and mingle that you no longer know you
are you or another, to constantly absorb and constantly radi-
ate, to double your personality in bestowing it—that is love."

There are those, of course, who find this exhilarating, not
just the result of it but the process itself. We did not. For me, it
was excruciating. For Jill, agonizing. My failure and my need
came as a flash of light, even though Jill had been trying to tell
me for a decade.

I realized that everything she had ever nagged about, complained about, pleaded about was true. I was broken. God allowed me to remember her every lament and to list these on
sheet after yellow sheet from a legal pad. I prayed that God
would use a wrecking ball on the marriage so it could start over
and begin as something new and whole.

Jill's ego, on the other hand, had been starved to death over
the course of the first ten years of the marriage, until she
thought there was nothing left. While this could have and
should have been avoided, we realize now, given the players in
the drama of our marriage, it had to happen.

Though Jill felt wronged by my insensitivity and misplaced
priorities, her ego, her love self, her solar plexus needed a
ruining that would put her at ground zero, able to truly love
and be loved.

GLOW WORDS

You can never be happily married until you get a divorce from yourself. Successful marriage means a certain death to self.

—Jerry McCant

The Bible says that when a man "takes a new wife, he shall not go out with the army, not be charged with any duty; he shall be free at home one year and shall give happiness to his wife whom he has taken" (Deuteronomy 24:5 NAS).

Most modern Christians smile when they hear that verse, amused by the impracticality of it for modern living. Marriage and family counselor Craig Massey thinks it might be more practical than we imagine. In a *Moody Monthly* article several years ago, he speculated on how much money might be made available to newlyweds if all their gifts were cash and all the wedding extras were dispensed with.

His point was that, practical or not, there had to be a good reason for that admonition to be included in the Scriptures. "The wedding day is important, of course," he writes. "But the wedding is an event. The marriage is a growing relationship. Marriage takes time. According to this verse, one year of twenty-four-hour-a-day association is necessary for the development of the union."

Massey makes the point that any wedding really involves four marriages: two minds, two sets of emotions, two bodies, and two spiritual souls. There is much to be learned, much to be probed.

These four dimensions do not result from a wedding, but from a continuing deepening of the two people as they cleave together. . . .

The greatest job of an intelligent man is to understand his

wife's responses to herself, to him, and to the world's influence upon her. Peter tells us that a woman is far more delicate than a man, and in Proverbs we find that her value goes beyond the most priceless gem. If a man knows nothing of the value of his wife, can he appreciate her?

. . . Husband hear this: You hold the key to a successful marriage. You are to love your wife as Christ loved the church and gave Himself for it. If you are willing to die for your wife, you should be willing to live for her.

The Bible doesn't say to marry the one you love, but it does say to love the one you marry.

Why? Why is the marital relationship so important? Because it is a reflection of God's love for the Church, Christ's bride.

A major factor in a good marriage, just as in a good relationship with a child, is knowledge. Knowing. Really knowing and understanding someone. There are no shortcuts, no gimmicks, no magic. To know someone, you need to invest time in talking and listening. Paying attention.

One of the best marriage books we came across during our marathon reading sessions was John Allan Lavender's *Marriage at Its Best* (Accent, 1982). He says that two hindrances to good communication that must be overcome are "the bad habits of lazy listening and hasty speaking. The confusion that results can be more tragic than comic.

". . . There's probably no better advice for both men and women than that which is given in James 1:19. 'Let everyone be quick to hear, slow to speak. . . .' "

It's a matter of love and friendship. What better friend and lover is there than one who cares enough about you to invest time with you, listening and sharing?

GLOW WORDS

A great marriage is 10 percent physical and 90 percent friendship.

—Dr. Paul Meier

Listening is a very conscious form of loving. I can't tell you how many times I used to talk to Pat and he'd say, "Yes, go ahead. I'm listening." But he'd go on reading the sports page, or I could tell his mind was still running through the score of a 76ers game. It didn't mean he didn't love me, but that's the way it felt. It was unconscious, lazy listening. Now he is conscious; he works at listening—he shows I'm worth the same effort as the agent he might be negotiating with on a million-dollar deal. He makes me feel valuable.

Lionel A. Whiston says it this way in *For Those in Love* (Abingdon, 1983): ". . . To listen is to be able to act from the other's situation rather than our own. Then a man, even though tired at the end of the day, will offer not scolding or advice but strong arms and warm words of love to the frantic mother. The wife, weary herself, will offer her flesh to the discouraged or fatigued husband that they may celebrate together."

There are three walls that come between husbands and wives that must be understood before they can be torn down, according to psychologist Dr. Ken Druck, in *The Secrets Men Keep* (Doubleday, 1985).

The first is the Wall of Mother, Druck says. He explains that a man's expectations about women are strongly influenced by his mother. A man must remember that "your mother and your wife are not in a contest. Love your mother as your mother and your wife as your wife."

The second is the Wall of Goddess Worship. This is usually a problem early on in the marriage when the husband thinks he has found the perfect woman. "But, of course, nobody's perfect. The goddess turns out to be grouchy in the morning—or she gains some weight. Then he feels disappointed and loses interest in her."

To tear down that wall, Dr. Druck says, "Stop being so critical. Make it a point to notice something new and positive every day about your wife. Don't be afraid to express your appreciation directly."

Third, there's the Wall of Anger. "Sometimes men secretly punish their wives for things their mothers or former girl-friends did. Often to prevent a similar injury, a man will put up this wall of anger. A man like this usually isn't even aware of how angry he is.

"The only way to tear down this wall is to face those feelings and how you're transferring them onto your partner. . . . It's important that we don't blame only men for these walls. . . . Men and women should work together to steadily dismantle these walls so they can share closer, more rewarding relation-ships."

There is an inherent danger in all this attention spouses can give each other. What happens if we listen and share so much that we really let our guards down and get to know each other? Will the illusion be gone? Will the lustre be lacking? Will we be aware of all the differences between us?

Yes.

GLOW WORDS

The most difficult and most essential task in marriage is learning which defects must be ig-nored and accepted in the other partner. Most unhappy marriages are created by trying to change what cannot be changed.

—Sydney J. Harris

The first of four steps to harmony, according to author Lionel Whiston, "is to recognize and admit these differences. 'My mate has a different temperament than I have and meets situations and problems in a different way than I do.' . . . Let us then frankly admit these differences in taste and temperament.

"In the second place, we need to set our mate free to be the kind of a person he or she is, to act and respond in the way that seems appropriate."

P.M.; and a mother of three added, "If I ever run away from home, I'll surely leave at 5:15 P.M."

This is a time of day when husband and wife can come to each other's rescue and give tangible evidence of their love and support. Many is the day a wife needs to protect a weary husband from a barrage of wound-up children and her own complaints. On the husband's side I used to think of this as a good time to make a grand entrance as the Father of the Family. Now I see it as a time when I can show Jill how much I love her by taking the kids off her hands, or assisting in the preparation of dinner, or whatever she needs most at the time.

There are other times when spouses can come to each other's rescue and show their mutual support. I love the story *You and Your Network* author Fred Smith tells about the father who discovered his two teenage sons hassling his wife to the point of tears.

> He walked up behind the two, grabbed them by their necks and bumped their heads together. The blow was just hard enough that they both fell to the floor with big knots rising on their foreheads.
>
> While they lay there, he said, "Stop hassling my woman! Fortunately for you, we were married before you got here, and fortunately for us, we're going to be married after you leave." Big tears ran down his wife's face, and those two boys learned a valuable lesson in the solidarity of parental authority.*

GLOW WORDS

An octogenarian obstetrician once told me that if the father's first question is, "Boy or girl?" he charges double what he would if the father's first question is, "How's my wife?"

—Bennett Cerf

---

* From *You and Your Network* by Fred Smith, copyright © 1984 by Fred Smith; used by permission of Word Books, Publisher, Waco, Texas.

A wife, of course, needs to have the same attitude about her husband. Louis M. Terman has been quoted: "If a wife does not love her husband more than she loves her children, both the children and the marriage are in danger."

This important matter of mutual support was discussed by Marilyn McGinnis in the January, 1984 issue of *Family Life Today.*

> A challenge to the commitment aspect of marriage is in the area of mutual support. At perhaps no other time in life do we as parents need as much encouragement and support from our mates as when we are trying to raise our children.
>
> Being a parent is tougher than any of us ever expected. It is also more rewarding than we could have known. But sometimes the rewards are long term—we have to go through a lot of hassle before the rewards appear. Along the way we are often filled with doubts, fears, frustration, and guilt. There are many times when we really don't know whether we have made the right decision or not.
>
> But the frustration of work and the demands of the children seem to fade when your spouse gives you a hug, a special look, or says, "Honey, I think you made a wise decision. I'm proud of you."
>
> Instead of supporting each other in the midst of their struggles, some people look for a way out. The "me first" philosophy is never far from us. They look around for a sexier partner, a romantic interlude, or a new and supposedly better marriage altogether.
>
> "In so doing," says Dr. James Dobson in his book *Straight Talk to Men and Their Wives,* "they leave in their wake former husbands or wives who feel rejected and bitter and unloved. They produce little children who crave the affection of a father or mother ... but never find it. All that is left on the march toward old age is a series of broken relationships and shattered lives and hostile children."

How can you encourage and support each other? In a million little thoughtful ways. Here is the start of a list that Jill and

I prepared one evening after the kids were in bed and we both needed to get a few things "down on paper." We call it our Loving by Doing List.

Pat's List

I can love you by ...
bringing you freshly squeezed orange juice in the morning

praising you in front of others for something you have done well

washing the dishes when you are too tired to clean up the kitchen

giving you a single, long-stemmed rose when you aren't expecting it

taking time out during the day to meet you for lunch

giving you my full attention when you want to talk to me

Jill's List

I can love you by ...
greeting you with enthusiasm when you come home at night

preparing your favorite meal instead of always catering to the kids' likes

learning more about the things you are interested in

backing you up when you have made a tough decision

not expecting you to read my mind and being hurt when you don't

not being overly critical and complaining

It doesn't take a vacation to Tahiti or a mink coat to give each other the support and encouragement that's needed each day. It *does* take caring enough to show love no matter what else is happening.

There was the weekend when Pat was the perfect father. He took the boys to their baseball practices Friday night, took the girls and little Michael for individual bike rides the next morning, watched the kids while I took a nap, and then took the whole family on an outing.

On Sunday after church, he took the four younger kids to

the playground and the older two to work out at a baseball diamond, then later took the three older to an NBA play-off game. Before bedtime he prepared, as usual, the sandwiches for all the lunches the next day.

Only when we were ready for bed did it occur to him that he might have been a good father at the expense of being a good husband. I had gotten the short end that weekend, but Pat will make it up to me another time. He knows now that balance is called for among his many tasks as husband and father. Moreover, I reminded him that by taking care of the kids, he was giving me a respite from the daily routine.

Speaking of the daily routine, remember to enjoy your kids. Jill focuses on the joys and rewards of child rearing to get her through the drudgery of certain mundane daily tasks. One practical approach, according to psychologist Arnie Medvene, is to turn the time spent on certain home tasks into a time of fun with the children: "Instead of immediately attacking the evening's work—dinner, cleanup, laundry, etc.,—first do something enjoyable outside of the house with the child, like take a walk, meet a neighbor, play ball."

What gets lost in the high-intensity, active American family is extra leisure time. Most of us assign a low priority to just plain having fun. Do kids care about your high-pressure, fast-track life? No. Howard Hendricks says that his kids have told him that what they remember most about him from their childhood was his wrestling with them on the floor. Are we fun enough as parents? As husbands and wives?

A lack of fun can be emotionally expensive, say other psychologists, causing stress in the family expressed in anger, withdrawal, or difficulty in responding to one's spouse or children.

An insidious side of marital discord is the way it can affect all parts of life. In late 1982, just before my D-Day confrontation with Pat, I got three speeding tickets. This was not normal for me, but it was such a period of upheaval in our lives I just wasn't myself. Then, when the marriage seemed to be on the verge of salvage, I was hurrying to pick up Pat and get to the plane taking us to a weekend in Florida and I was ticketed again. My license was suspended for a time and we paid several hundred dollars a year for three years in surcharges on our insurance. I'm confident nothing like this will happen again, but the scars of marital strife remain in reminders such as this: Another ticket could result in a thirty-to-sixty-day suspension of my license.

We don't have all the answers. Occasionally there are episodes showing that our marriage still isn't perfect—just normal. And that's worth remembering, because the ideal of a "perfect marriage" is the enemy of a good marriage. Particularly when we have been asked to speak or sing somewhere, it seems Satan tries for a field day with us. With an extra load on a busy schedule, we'll start sniping at each other or losing patience. Satan would love to have us lose the victory in our relationship and feel like hypocrites telling how the Lord brought us back together. That's when we have to step back and remind each other what is happening and commit our relationship to the Lord.

Not long ago we planned a night out at a nice restaurant. I got all gussied up, but Pat chose not to wear a tie. I tried hard to suppress my displeasure, but it finally burst forth: "You saw me dressing up! Why no tie?"

Without a word Pat opened the car door. "Where are you going?" I asked.

"To put on a tie, what else?"

"Forget it! Not if I have to tell you!"

But Pat went in and put one on anyway. Both of us were quiet during dinner. Finally, by the time dessert came, the tension began to ease and I thought about the silliness of the whole thing. What a waste! Two grown people ruining a good meal by sulking over a necktie. I burst out laughing and Pat laughed too. Such an incident in the past might have lasted three days with a full-blown silent treatment and all. Now, we were able to poke fun at ourselves.

We feel we've come a long way on the road to marital friendship. You can, too. We learned, the hard way, that building a solid marriage and a strong, rewarding family life depends on putting your priorities in order—and keeping them there. It's as simple as 1 Corinthians 13.

Chapter Two

Priorities

> Both parents should impose self-discipline upon themselves with respect to their own routines. Time should be scheduled to be spent with the children. Even if communication and approachability are good, the child or adolescent needs to know that he can spend time regularly with both his parents on particular occasions. ... This demands time spent together, doing things together; not merely cohabiting in the same house.
> —O. Quentin Hyder, *The People You Live With*

Can we lay to rest once and for all one of the most insidious myths to come along in the last fifteen years? You've heard it. It's the blather about spending quality time with your family if you don't have a large quantity of time.

Someone came up with this idea to salve the consciences of men and women who put their careers, their social lives, their projects ahead of their families. Dads would say, "But this is a crucial time in my career. I have to work sixty-hour weeks to get ahead, to climb the corporate ladder, to make more money, to provide for my family."

The end seemed honorable enough, but were the wishes of the wife and kids ever considered? Perhaps son and daughter needed love and attention and self-esteem and dad more than they needed a beautiful home and the latest fashions, gadgets, and creature comforts. They need a little 1 Corinthians 13 love.

What is quality time to a toddler? Little kids don't want to sit

41

with mom or dad for twenty minutes and discuss the cosmos.
They want attention, time, blocks of time. They want to climb
on you, wrestle with you, be tickled by you, held, stroked,
talked to. The same is true for wives who are "widows" to their
husband's jobs, as Jill was during the earlier years of our marriage. The response to *Rekindled* indicates that there are many
wives out there longing for "quantity time" with their husbands.

In *If I Were Starting My Family Again* (Abingdon, 1979),
John M. Drescher relates an incident that brought home to
him the importance of spending time with a small child:

> One night I was about asleep when I heard footsteps in the
> hall. Three-year-old David came slowly through the doorway
> and stood by my bed.
> "What do you want, David?"
> "Nothing, Daddy. I wanted to crawl in beside you and talk
> a little."
> I pulled the covers back and in he came. He snuggled there
> in silence a short time and then said, "Daddy, it was fun
> holding your hand in front of that lion's cage."
> "It sure was. Were you scared?"
> "Just a little bit."
> After another short time of silence, David said, "We really
> had a good time together today, didn't we, Daddy?"
> "We sure did."
> And that was all. David threw the covers back and went
> quickly to his own room. He was soon sound asleep. But I re-
> mained awake for some time. My small son awakened me
> anew to the importance of taking time to be together as a
> family.

When John Foster Dulles was United States Secretary of
State, he once phoned the home of General Douglas Mac-
Arthur. Mrs. MacArthur mistook him for an aide and snapped,
"MacArthur is where MacArthur always is, weekdays, Satur-
days, Sundays, and nights—in that office!" Within minutes,
MacArthur got a telephoned order from Dulles: "Go home at
once, boy. Your home front is crumbling."

One of the most poignant pieces ever written about the high cost of misplaced priorities and the resultant model they present is Harry and Sandy Chapin's "Cat's in the Cradle."

My child arrived just the other day
he came to the world in the usual way—
But there were planes to catch and bills to pay
he learned to walk while I was away
And he was talkin' 'fore I knew it and as he grew he'd say
I'm gonna be like you, Dad
you know I'm gonna be like you.

And the cat's in the cradle and the silver spoon
Little boy blue and the man in the moon
When you comin' home, Dad
I don't know when
but we'll get together then—
you know we'll have a good time then

My son turned 10 just the other day
he said, Thanks for the ball, Dad, c'mon let's play
Can you teach me to throw? I said not today
I got a lot to do. He said, That's okay
And he walked away but his smile never dimmed
it said I'm gonna be like him, yeah
you know I'm gonna be like him

Well he came home from college just the other day
so much like a man I just had to say
Son, I'm proud of you, can you sit for awhile
He shook his head and said with a smile—
What I'd really like, Dad, is to borrow the car keys
See you later, can I have them please?

And the cat's in the cradle and the silver spoon
Little boy blue and the man in the moon
When you comin' home, Son?
I don't know when
but we'll get together then
you know we'll have a good time then

I've long since retired, my son's moved away
I called him up just the other day
I said I'd like to see you if you don't mind
He said I'd love to, Dad—if I can find the time
You see my new job's a hassle and the kids have the flu
but it's sure nice talkin' to you, Dad
It's been nice talking to you

And as I hung up the phone it occurred to me—
he'd grown up just like me
My boy was just like me

And the cat's in the cradle and the silver spoon
Little boy blue and the man in the moon
When you comin' home, Son?
I don't know when
but we'll get together then, Dad
we're gonna have a good time then

The problem with trying to substitute quality for quantity
time with an older child is that it may take hours of being with
him before he feels free to really open up. You could carve out
thirty minutes from your busy schedule for "quality" time and
ask dozens of questions, only to get one-syllable responses.
Talking with a child is different from interrogating him. Real
time invested in a child involves just being with him, maybe
not saying anything for long stretches.

◊ GLOW WORDS

Quality time can seldom be planned. Special
moments are like seeds. They must be planted
and watered before you can expect them to
grow. Then be ready to stop and enjoy the
flowers—when they come.

—Patricia H. Rushford
What Kids Need Most in a Mom

This time could be invested while riding in the car to his activities, spending a day doing what he or she wants to do. Sometimes the real closeness, the true opening up, comes during the last few minutes of the day when you're putting your child to bed.

He feels at ease with you because he's been with you for a long period. He has seen you laugh and have fun. He knows your heart is tender toward him. He's not sitting at the kitchen table under bright lights being asked how school was. He's not being asked anything. Maybe he's simply being told, by word or action, that you care about him, treasure him, are proud of him, are glad he's your child.

In the peaceful, low light of his bedroom, he may just come out with something you need to know, something you can help with, or just something that gives you a clear insight into his character, which will help you be a better parent.

Parents who think they're doing the job by scheduling their kids the way they schedule board meetings or shopping trips will miss out on intimate times like that. Kids know when they are being fitted in. "Okay, I can help you with your project for twenty minutes, but then I have to make a phone call" tells a child precisely where he stands.

A good family life takes time. There is no substitute for it. And both husband and wife need to enlarge their circle of love and commitment. Once we realized the enormous benefits to our marriage of the B-E-S-T principles, we started working together to apply them to our children. We saw almost immediate dramatic changes in their schoolwork, their relationships with each other, and with us.

Let's not kid ourselves. When we put work and social life ahead of the children, it's because those are our values. The kids *are* indeed second place. Don't like to admit that? Look at your schedule.

We say our families are important, that they are first place with us. Then we find that we have spent a total of an hour with a child in a week. Where does he rank in reality?

Obviously, most breadwinners have to spend at least forty

hours a week on the job, and another few hours getting back and forth to work. That leaves only a few hours a day between arriving home and when the kids go to bed. Children don't expect more than that. They don't expect you to go to school with them or be with them all day every day of the summer.

All they want is some proof of what you say. You say they are more important to you than anyone else in the world. Does that fact make you say no to your boss if he asks a favor? If you had planned to take your kids to a ball game one Saturday and your boss called on your way out the door, what would you do?

"It's a big one, Steve. We've been trying to land this account for months and the guy's coming in on an eleven o'clock flight. If you could pick him up, take him to lunch, and get him settled in his hotel, I know we could get the account. It would be credited to you and the entire commission for the next year would be yours. Could amount to thousands. Can I count on you?"

What would you say? We didn't imply it was going to be easy.

You might have to decide whether telling your boss that you couldn't do it because of your commitment to your kids would cost you your job. Of course, your kids are more important than your job, but you need an income to feed them too. You know your boss. What would he say?

Another option might be to consult with the children, if they are old enough to understand the ramifications of their advice. You can tell them that you're in a bind, that you want to make good on your promise and that you will if they want you to. If they would rather you do what your boss is asking, you could make it up to them later. The benefit here is that by involving them in the decision, you're implying that they are every bit as important to you as your job.

They are also getting the opportunity to be more loving, more considerate, more understanding, and more flexible than your boss. Let them see how difficult the decision is for you, and make it clear that your preference is to fulfill your obligation to the family.

You'll find them surprisingly understanding and they'll likely make the wisest choice, eager to make your life easier. But if you can tell from body language or the looks in their eyes that to renege on your commitment—even temporarily—would cause more trouble than it's worth, you have a big decision to make.

One way to head off this kind of no-win situation is to let your boss know in advance that your family is a very high priority and that there will be times when you have made commitments with them that you cannot break.

You can do the same with your children. Tell them they are top priority and that nine times out of ten nothing will get in the way of your commitments. But there might be rare exceptions over which you have no control, but for which you will compensate in some other way. This is part of their maturing process, to learn that things don't *always* go off without a hitch.

The story is told that one time Bill Gaither turned down an offer to play and sing for then United States President Gerald Ford. Apparently when the call came, Gaither checked his calendar and declined, explaining, "I'm scheduled to be home with the family."

Bill explains: "When you set your priorities and say, 'Not even the president is going to take me away from this,' you will have time to be a father. And if you do not, good things will just keep eating away at your effectiveness and family life."

Keeping our word to our children is so very important. But, of course, obstacles do come up to interfere with our plans. But when this happens—deal with it! Anticipate the disappointment, acknowledge the problem, explain, even apologize if necessary. Just don't ignore it. Avoiding uncomfortable situations can be damaging to a child—or a spouse—because it appears that we don't care.

We learned recently that the average cost of feeding, clothing, and educating a firstborn child is more than a quarter of a million dollars. Doesn't it seem that before a person would make such an investment, he would research it, watch it, nurture it, tend it?

No other so costly outlay of cash would be treated as a low priority item in our lives.

Priorities overlap with modeling. You can model a good marriage by letting your children know that you keep your commitments to your spouse, too. There will be times when even they should not interfere with that time, even if it just consists of the two of you watching a favorite old movie on television together or sitting in the family room for a half-hour chat.

It seems there have never been more middle-aged Christian parents with regrets than there are now. Everywhere you look and listen you see and hear people with bad cases of the "if onlys." If only we had spent more time on the important things. If only I had gotten closer to my son. If only we had been more affectionate, told our daughter we loved her, given her a hug every day, taken her with us on trips.

◍ GLOW WORDS

Because they are fragile, handling children with care is essential. You'll be glad you did when all you have is an old photo and the memory of a package God delivered into your care many, many years ago.

—Charles Swindoll
Growing Strong in the Seasons of Life

Husbands regret the ways in which they take their wives for granted too. A big league baseball player told me that after he read *Rekindled,* he realized the truth in what his wife had been saying for years. She resented having to stay home and raise the children and do all the work while he played ball, traveled, had fun, and enjoyed getting the accolades that go with doing a good job.

"It wasn't that she didn't want to be a housewife and mother," he explained. "She just needed some strokes, and she needed them from me. She does her job as well as I do mine, and hers is tougher. She can keep it up and stay at the task, if I bless and edify her."

He told me he had been applying those principles and that the next several weeks were "fantastic."

Zig Ziglar, in *Raising Positive Kids in a Negative World*, tells the story of Fritz Kreisler, the world-famous violinist, who was once approached by an enthusiastic music fan. She cried, "Mr. Kreisler, I'd give my life to play as you do!"

"Madam," he quietly replied, "I did."

Ziglar adds, "I am not suggesting you have to give your life to raise a positive child, but I am suggesting that you're going to have to give many hours."

So many people, particularly men, wish they had it to do over. "This time I would spend less time in the office and more time at home. I would take it easier, be warmer, be more friendly, talk more, listen more, be more attentive."

But it's too late. The kids are grown and gone, and they're distant, not only geographically. They still get together occasionally, but either there's a silent tension or awkwardness, or there is open sibling warfare, the way there was in the home for years.

One father, in *The Fulfilled Family,* summed it up this way. He said, "My family's all grown, and the kids are all gone. But if I had it to do over, this is what I'd do:

1. I would love my wife more in front of my children.
2. I would laugh with my children more—at our mistakes and our joys.
3. I would listen more, even to the littlest child.
4. I would be more honest about my own weaknesses, never pretending perfection.
5. I would pray differently for my family—instead of focusing on their shortcomings, I'd focus on mine.

6. I would do more things together with my children.

7. I would encourage them more and bestow more praise.

8. I would pay more attention to little things, like deeds and words of thoughtfulness.

9. I would share God more intimately with my family. Every ordinary thing that happened in every ordinary day I would use to direct them to God.

One of the things we want to avoid at all cost in the Williams household is regrets. With all the books and tapes and articles and films on the subject, no parent who's currently in the thick of the battle should have any excuse. We *can* avoid the regrets and the "if onlys" if we act now.

It's not too late if your kids are still at home. True, it might shock a high school senior if all of a sudden she was listened to and hugged and put high on the priority list. But for her time remaining at home, you can convince her of your sincerity. They will be the most memorable months of her childhood and will pave the way for a satisfying adult relationship.

But if your children are younger, you have the chance to revolutionize your home by rearranging your priorities. An announcement might be necessary, something to keep you on your toes. You might say to your children, "Kids, we have an announcement to make. We have always considered you the most important people in our lives, but we haven't known how to prove it by showing it. From now on we want to prove we mean it by acting like it. We're going to tell you what we think that means, and then we want you to tell us what you think we can do to make it obvious."

That doesn't mean that discipline and appropriate punishment goes out the window, or that you turn the kids into fun junkies by providing for their every whim. In fact, it may mean some cracking down on television viewing, curfews, homework, manners. More emphasis on all those things is proof of love too, but you'd better warn them in advance.

Is housework a higher priority than your children? Are you so concerned with keeping a tidy home that your children feel trapped inside a magazine cover? Within reason, which is more important? Is it not their home and furniture as much as it is yours?

That doesn't mean they should be allowed to jump on and climb over and ruin good furniture. They can learn proper care for nice things as part of your new priorities. But rooms will get messy when kids play in them. Milk will be spilled at the table. Furniture will wear out faster. Decide what you're raising. Rooms or children?

GLOW WORDS

Cleaning your house while your children are still growing is like shoveling the walk before it stops snowing.

—Phyllis Diller

Other mothers frequently ask me how I do it. Raising six kids, the wife of a busy husband, carrying on a ministry, cutting records, and so forth. They say, "I have only two children and I can't seem to find time for anything else."

I feel I have less time to waste, and so I try not to waste it. I'm a list person, know in advance what needs to be done each day, and set about doing it. It's the little insidious things that rob time. Soap operas, women's magazines, gossiping, whatever. People find time to do what they really want to do.

Perhaps a parent's *top* priority ought to be prayer. Prayer for and prayer with your children. We know of a woman who prayed for her children before she was even pregnant! She knew she and her husband would be having children, adopting them if necessary, so she began praying for whomever the first little one was that God would send her way.

She prayed that he or she would come to a saving knowledge of Jesus Christ and that he or she would grow up in love with the Lord and desiring to serve Him.

When she became pregnant, she prayed for the eventual potential spouse of her unborn child. "If he is a boy," she prayed, "please prepare for him a woman who loves You, Father, a woman who is a Christian and will share his faith, a woman who will support him in his service to You. And if my child is a girl, prepare for her a man who will be godly and righteous and who will love her as You love Your church."

That's one way to avoid regrets!

Of course, this mother prayed for her children after they were born too. She prayed for them every day, not just for their safety at school and on their way to and from, but also for their futures. Jill keeps school and activity calendars at her desk and prays for each child during the appropriate time slot.

Paul Lewis, in *How Can a Father Win?* (American Tract Society), tells the story of Sam, a young Christian whose hunger for spiritual growth was evidenced by the notes and remarks he wrote in the margins of his Bible. So he felt he had lost a part of himself when he discovered his Bible was missing after a camping trip in Oregon.

Five years later, Sam was moving a box of books for parents of a Christian young lady he was seriously dating, when a book tumbled out of the box and flipped over onto the floor. There lay Sam's long-lost Bible.

While camping years earlier, the girl's family had found the Bible with no identification but "Sam" on the cover. Impressed with the spiritual insights reflected in the marginal notes, the parents' prayer since then had been, "God, please send a man to marry our daughter who loved you like 'Sam.' "

Your prayers will provide what your children need!

It's easier to pray for children than to pray with them, unless you start when they are very young. It's the same as saying, "I love you." Did you say that to your parents and did they say it to you? If not, you probably still don't trade that tender comment to this day. And don't you wish you could? You love each other, but you can't say it.

Pray with your children or you'll find yourself in the same

predicament with prayer. It's so easy, and so sweet to the child. When they are hurt or angry or afraid, ask them if they'd like you to pray about it right now. Even if they shake their head no, say, "I want to. Let's bow our heads. Dear God, thank you for giving Mary to me. You know how much I love her and I'm glad you made me her parent. Please help me be a good one and do whatever You want me to, to help her grow up healthy and happy and loving you. I pray that you'll help her not be afraid when the lightning flashes and the thunder rolls, because these are just part of your plan to give the thirsty plants and trees and grass enough water to grow."

Praying for our children is only the beginning of our responsibility for creating a spiritual environment for them at home. For every Christian parent, leading a child to love and desire to serve the Lord is a top priority.

Chapter Three

Creating a Spiritual Environment

> ... **Bring them up in the training and instruction of the Lord.**
>
> Ephesians 6:4 NIV

We have a lovely old colonial house across the river from Philadelphia with beautiful old trees around it. It is Jill's pride and her renovation project. But what makes the house lovely is the kids who make the house the home. We have a houseful of kids and we wouldn't have it any other way. Jill always wanted to be "just a plain ol' mother," and to her, the more the merrier. Only reluctantly and slowly did I come around to this point of view, but now a busy, noisy house is as natural to me as it is to Jill.

Jim was born in May of 1974. He's a quiet, fun-loving kid who takes a lot of responsibility for his little brothers and sisters.

Bob, born in June of 1977, is outgoing and loves to laugh, but he's also deep and can be touching. I experienced his sensitivity one night earlier this year. I returned home late after the rest of the family had gone to bed and on my desk I found a note addressed to "Number 1 Dad." It was handwritten, a typical mix of printing and script by an eight-year-old, on a folded sheet of construction paper. It read:

54

Dead Dad,

I really appreciate you being my dad. I am really happy that your my dad. Because you put me to bed. You have catches with me. You help me with school work. You play basketball with me. You take me to school and to basketball games. Out of the whole world, you are the only Dad I would pick to be my Dad.

I am really enjoying school My favorite subject is math and spelling. Art also.

You are the Number 1 Dad because you do everything with me. I have to go now. See you tomorrow.

Love, Bob.

Karyn was a July, 1979, baby and likes to copy Jill in everything from mannerisms to singing. We were told that Sarah and Andrea, our Korean children, were born in July of 1980 and 1981 respectively, but such things are hard to pin down. If we had to guess, we'd put their ages even closer; it's even possible they're twins. They're incredibly affectionate and good-natured, but also independent when they want to be.

Michael was born to us in June of 1984, and from the moment he started crawling, it's been a whole new world for us. He goes a mile a minute from sunup to sundown, running, jumping, picking, poking, nosing. He's the first child who's caused us to put valuables out of reach.

Needless to say, we're all up early with plenty of chores, washing up, brushing teeth, dressing, feeding, and getting off to school and work. There are a few hours of more controlled chaos when it's just Mom and Michael, but otherwise, the action doesn't stop until all the kids are in bed.

Jill loves it. "I miss them when they're away, and my day is complete when they're all back home." She has a sign on the wall that reads, "Dull women have immaculate homes."

Of course we think our kids are the most beautiful and talented with whom God ever chose to bless the world, and there's little we want more than to see them happy and successful. But there is *one* thing more.

We want our kids all to become Christians and be assured of
heaven, and we want them to lead the abundant life Jesus talks
about in John 10:10. That doesn't mean they must all become
preachers, evangelists, or missionaries, though that would thrill
us as much as if they became sports superstars or Miss
Americas.

It does mean that we want to see them develop a loving,
daily relationship with Christ now so that as they mature,
communing with God will be the most natural thing in their
lives. We learned a long time ago that this will not happen au-
tomatically.

We cannot count on having spiritually alive Christian children simply because they are involved in church and Sunday
school or because they attend Christian schools. We're happy
that they are and that they do, but the admonition is *ours* to
train up a child in the way he should go.

That means we must set the spiritual tone. We must be the
examples, the models for our children. Otherwise, we might be
troubling our house, and Scripture is clear that "He who trou-
bles his own house will inherit the wind" (Proverbs 11:29 NAS).

We don't really know what it means to "inherit the wind,"
but it sure doesn't sound like inheriting eternal life, does it? We
don't want to find out. We have committed ourselves to raising
a godly family and making whatever sacrifices that might require.

That doesn't mean we are overconfident or have all the answers. If we did, we wouldn't be reading every book on the
subject that comes down the pike. Neither do we attempt to
share any wisdom about raising teenagers. Jim will be a teenager soon, so talk to us in ten years or so when the whole clan
has dragged us through adolescence.

For now, we want to create a spiritual environment, a place
where God is talked about and worshiped, a place where we
think and talk about Jesus Christ and what He would do if He
were in our places. Better yet, we want our kids to know and
understand that Jesus *is* in our places, and has been since the
Cross.

GLOW WORDS

Only in the home can children see living models of Christ reflecting Him in the midst of daily living. Only in the home are there time and experience enough to mold human nature into Christian character.

—Lois E. LeBar
Family Devotions with School-Age Children

The spiritual life of the family can't be overemphasized. Entire books have been written on the subject, and many more probably need to be written. What good is raising a child who is bright and articulate and successful and even seemingly happy if he is lost for eternity and never enjoys a relationship with God, either now or in the hereafter?

And don't let anyone tell you that spiritually minded families break up at the same rate as secular ones. Research shows that among marriages where the couples attend church regularly, study the Bible, and pray together, only one in four hundred marriages ends in divorce. In society at large, one in two marriages breaks up.

Francis and Edith Schaeffer are two of our heroes of the faith, not just because of their erudite thinking and love for young, searching minds, but also for the example they set as Christian parents. We were privileged to aid in promoting one of the late Dr. Schaeffer's film series in our area. What a thrill it was to meet him and to see his love for Christ shine in his daily life. Praying as we rode along in the car was as natural to him as conversing with someone.

(How pleased we were recently when our own Andrea was riding with Jill in the car. It was a hot day and the sunroof was open. At a stoplight, Andrea unbuckled her seat belt, stood, and poked her head out the top, and said, "Hi, Jesus!" Just like Dr. Schaeffer!)

We admired the Schaeffers' five rules to strengthen the family, about which Francis spoke and wrote so often. Any parents with the desire and the discipline to follow these guidelines can be certain to raise unique children, blessed of God. So Jill asked him about them.

"First, Jill," he said, "commit your family to a life of prayer." There should be daily prayer, individually and together, committing everything to God and trusting Him to meet even the smallest needs. Such a discipline undoubtedly led to his own natural way of praying anywhere, anytime, and you can be sure that rubbed off on his children.

"Pat, fathers often feel that they have to be the authority figure in the house, but remember this: Make the Bible your final authority not only in matters of theology, but in every area of life, faith, practice, history, and ethics." The only standards for living are those that can be supported by Scripture.

"It may sound funny to you, but I love Scripture so much, I've found myself quite unconsciously waking up in the morning and reaching over to pat my Bible affectionately."

"Third, Jill, we emphasize creativity in our family. And I sense you're the creative, artistic person in your family. Our children are writers, painters, filmmakers, because we've tried to transform even mundane tasks into things of beauty that glorified God.

"Both of you need to hold this fourth point in your hearts: We believe our children are gifts of infinite value and therefore we have made them full and responsible partners in the family. This allowed our children to share their deepest doubts and questions without fear of rejection.

"And, fifth, we believe in the sanctity and the beauty of marriage. To us, the two partners in God's union live one life to the fullest in a complementary relationship of love and commitment."

That experience with the Schaeffers became a true source of

inspiration for us. We knew that to emulate the strengths of the Schaeffer home, we would have to take lessons from their marriage as well. We would have to find ways to be alone together, to really get to know each other, to build faith and trust in each other, to become best friends.

A key verse for us became Proverbs 24:3, 4: "By wisdom a house is built, and by understanding it is established; and by knowledge the rooms are filled with all precious and pleasant riches" (NAS).

Formulating spiritual goals for the family is an essential first step—but just that, a first step. Any Christian parent would agree on the importance of acquainting children with prayer and Scripture reading and memorization. But how many become proficient in these areas themselves?

GLOW WORDS

If your relationship with Jesus Christ is vital, your family will know it. They will know it, not by your professional utterances, but by your love, your willingness to listen to an idea different from your own, your patience, your personal honesty, your obedience. It's contagious when it is authentic.

—Gladys M. Hunt, *Focus on Family Life*

Start by praying for your children. You might be surprised at how attitudes change, nerves calm, noise levels diminish. One woman said she discovered "that the children's temperaments (and my own) improved in direct proportion to my faithful prayer vigil on their behalf."

We all want to communicate to our families the importance of a daily quiet time, but do we have one ourselves? Evangelist Dwight L. Moody once wrote: "I prayed for faith, and thought that some day faith would come down and strike me like lightning. But faith did not seem to come. One day I read in the tenth chapter of Romans, 'Now faith cometh by hearing, and hearing by the Word of God.' I had closed my Bible, and prayed for faith. I now opened my Bible and began to study, and faith has been growing ever since."

Stuart P. Boehming, writing in *Discipleship Journal*, declares: "I have become absolutely convinced that having a daily devotional time with God is the single most important thing a Christian can do. It can keep him spiritually fit and morally prepared to face the storms of life, prepare him to be God's warrior and champion in this world, and draw him closer to God. At the end of the day there is nothing more important he can say than, 'I had my time with God.' "

Although it's important to develop a devotional time that meets *your own* needs and circumstances, here are some suggestions culled from our experience and that of others.

1. *Devotional time should be on a daily basis.* Better five minutes a day than one hour once a week. In fact, the busier and more pressured you are, the more important and rewarding is time spent with God. Consider Jesus' own example. The more demands that were placed on Him, the more He got away and spent time alone in prayer.

2. *Be realistic.* Don't start off by setting up a lengthy program that will be difficult to maintain.

3. *Include the reading of the Word.* Even a brief passage can help you discern God's counsel.

4. *Find what works best for you.* Some people find it essential to have their quiet time at the same hour and same place every day. Some prefer flexibility—spontaneously taking advantage of the outdoors to praise and thank God for a beautiful day, for example. Flexibility should be kept within the framework of daily commitment, however.

5. *Be honest in your communication with God.* Sometimes speaking with the Lord in a conversational way is a valuable adjunct to more formal prayer. It may free you to set before Him matters otherwise ignored. Remember, He is ready to minister to all your needs.

6. *Keep a journal.* Writing down prayer requests ahead of

time helps you to think them through. Sometimes we need reminding to keep praying about certain of our own traits. And keeping a record of the answers to prayer can be instructive and encouraging in the future.

7. *Take time to listen for God's message.* Too often we use our quiet time with God to do all the talking. We must make part of our quiet time just that—quiet time for listening for His guidance.

If you have tried to establish a devotional time and have not been successful, considering these questions may help you:

1. *Have you made a quiet time with God a top priority?* You will need to commit yourself to a conscious effort to take the time every day. You cannot rely, especially at first, on your feelings and inclinations.

2. *Have you stayed with it long enough?* Give yourself at least two months to establish a devotional time as a habit.

3. *Have you asked God's help about your commitment to this time?* This might well be the most important matter to bring before Him at the start.

4. *Are you expecting God to conform to your timetable?* It's important to realize that the benefits of quiet time in general and the answers to specific questions in particular may take time.

5. *Are you spending time in His Word?* Learn to depend on the whole counsel of God.

6. *Are you heeding God's counsel?* Your quiet time with God will not yield the rewards it should if you don't obey Him during the rest of the day.

The point of all this, of course, is to start or restart your own personal quiet time, not only for the benefit of your spiritual life, but also so you won't be a hypocrite when you encourage your children to do the same.

In 1975 Pat became convicted of his need to invest in serious Bible study and he committed himself to an hour a day. He read, he studied, he used commentaries, he took notes. Believe it or not, it became a sore spot in our marriage. I found myself jealous and resentful of the time he devoted to that while

I would have given anything for ten minutes of his uninterrupted time.

Four years later, Pat added the commitment to memorize a verse of Scripture a day to his already overcrowded schedule. He benefited from it, of course, but again, here was a near obsession that made his commitment to me look as pale as it was.

When our marriage was rescued in 1983, it became clear that some good things can actually have a bad effect when priorities are out of whack and other things are being neglected. The toughest thing I had to deal with when I felt neglected and rejected was that I couldn't complain about the specific activities in Pat's life that crowded me out.

Who would sympathize with a woman because her husband was at the top of his profession? Or that he was a physical fitness buff who exercised and jogged up to an hour a day? Or that he spoke to Christian groups all over the country? Or that he spent an hour a day in the Word and memorized Scripture besides?

Of course, now that our marriage has been rekindled, those elements of his life remain important to Pat. But they have been put in proper perspective. I'm now included, and sometimes the hour's Bible study is limited to a half-hour for the sake of marital communication.

We want our children to pray, read their Bibles, learn to study, and memorize Scripture. We've learned that what goes into our minds eventually issues in actions. Therefore, we believe that what you put into your mind and heart becomes the "printout" of your life to people around you.

If you don't like the way your children behave, change what they put in their heads. Fill their memory banks with Holy Scripture. Jill has mentioned my commitment to memorizing Scripture. From that experience I have learned ways to power that memorization and I've outlined them here. They can help you and your kids too.

1. *Believe you can.* You will be successful at memorizing something if you're convinced that it's important. What's more important than God's word?

2. *Be systematic.* Set a time each day for memorizing your Scripture verses. (I write verses on three-by-five cards and study them as I jog. Then I fasten them to the sun visor in my car and review them on my way to work.)

3. *Don't just memorize words.* Try to understand what the verses say—and then think about how they relate to you. Also relate them to other Bible passages.

4. *Use mental pictures.* Picture the verse itself in your mind and/or link the verse in your mind with a particular visual image. (I sometimes link a verse with a person. More about that later.)

5. *Follow a periodic system of reviewing* the verses so that you retain them.

The Navigators are probably the world's leading proponents of Scripture memorization, thus so much of the helpful material we've found on the subject comes from their magazine, the *Discipleship Journal.* In a recent issue there was an article by Lorne Sanny, until recently the general director of The Navigators, called "Five Reasons Why I Memorize Scripture." I want to share some of the highlights with you.

Deliverance from Sin. God's Word protects me from sin when it's hidden in my heart, making it available for the Holy Spirit to bring it to my mind.

Victory over Satan. Three times Jesus used this weapon to gain victory over Satan in the wilderness (Matthew 4:1–10). We, too, can have victory if we are equipped. Scripture memory puts the sword in the hand where we can use it.

Spiritual Prosperity. The Word is our food, and Scripture memory puts the food in our minds where it can nourish us.

Personal Guidance. Because I memorize Scripture, verses often come to my mind, giving me practical guidance on what to do.

Helping Others. God gives us His Word as a tool for helping others, and memorizing it puts it immediately at hand so that we can make the best use of it.

We don't always have our Bibles with us when we need deliverance, victory, guidance, or a truth to help others. But Scripture memory puts the Word in our hearts, food in our minds, a light on our path, a weapon in one hand, and a tool in the other.

Keeping the Bible at the top of our reading lists is essential. Yes, we should read Christian books, but not rely on them at the expense of the Bible. Hannelore Bozeman makes the point forcefully: "If Christian literature substitutes for the Word, it does to us spiritually what junk food does physically; it spoils the appetite without providing proper nutrients for growth."

Good marriages grow from commitment—especially when parenting is underway. Likewise, spiritual parenting grows from commitment, especially when a good marriage is underway. This idea of modeling Christ before our children is a huge undertaking, intimidating really. Yet it's our assignment.

In chapter five we deal with affirming our children through praising them, in much the same way we praise our spouses—in private and in public. But it's one thing to praise a child and quite another to teach him to praise God.

Ever think about how natural it is to accept praise? Mark Twain said he could go two months on a good compliment. But try telling a child that someone else deserves praise. We're born egotists, let's face it. From as far back as we can remember, we either wanted all the praise or we compared ourselves to the one receiving it.

Praise a child for getting a hit in a ball game and his brother will say, "*I* hit a homer!" It's the way we are. But there is a place to begin teaching children to praise someone else—their brothers and sisters, and specifically God.

In our house we often use conversational prayer. If you've never tried it, it may take some getting used to. Just sit together as a family and talk to God as if He were right there, a friend, a member of the family. Don't be irreverent, and close your eyes and bow your heads if that makes you concentrate better.

But just talk to God conversationally, one sentence at a time. Make it spontaneous. Children can learn important concepts about God as their personal friend this way. One might start, "Lord, we love you."

Another, "Thank you for protecting us on the way to school and work today."

"Thank you for being a God who never changes."

"Thank you for loving us."

"Thank you for giving us a great mom and for all the things she does for us."

"Please help Mr. Smith get well."

Our children should see and hear us pray, not just at mealtimes, or even just when we're having family or private devotions. If a family is conversant with God in sentence prayers, they will talk with Him about anything anytime. If a child gets hurt or scared or is disappointed or angry, it can become as natural as anything else to suggest praying right then and there.

Be careful not to make your private devotions so private that your kids don't even know you have them. If you're in a regular, systematized study of the Bible, do it at the kitchen or dining room table occasionally. Don't do it for show, but let the children become aware that it's a regular thing with you.

A friend of ours was playing a game with other teens at a Bible camp one dark summer night, running and chasing one another, when he came upon the cabin of the camp director. Our friend peeked in the lighted window and saw the director on his knees, his Bible open on the bed. The director was just as devout in private as he seemed to be in public, and that image was never forgotten.

◎ GLOW WORDS
Parenting is taking live wires and making sure they are well grounded.

If you conduct your own Bible study in front of your children occasionally, they may want to interrupt or even join in. You have to decide on the relative merits of that, keeping in mind the content of the material and the age of the child.

But if it is not convenient or appropriate to involve your

child in your own devotions, try scheduling a time, maybe aside from family devotions, where just two of you can enjoy reading Scripture together.

Too many kids grow up in Christian homes where the Bible is carried to church on Sunday and left on the shelf during the week. *Gimme that weekend religion, gimme that weekend religion. It was good enough for papa* . . .

Bobby has always been concerned about Sarah's and Andrea's salvation. When he asks us if they're going to heaven, we always remind him that he can tell them all about it. He can find out if what they are hearing from us and from Sunday school and family devotions is making any sense to them.

One day Jill discovered Karyn sitting on the landing at the top of the stairs. "Where's Bobby?"

Karyn pointed to Bobby's room. "Talking with Sarah about Jesus."

If we want to communicate that the Bible is what we know it to be—the Word of God—we have to prove it. We can't say one thing and do another. The Bible says that "These commandments that I give you today are to be upon your hearts" (Deuteronomy 6:6 NIV).

One of the most beautiful stories is one that appeared in the December, 1984 *Moody Monthly,* by H. Dennis Fisher, a Baptist minister, telling how he and his then seven-year-old daughter, Sarah, tasted the sweetness of the Word together. (Psalms 19:10 says the Word of God is "sweeter than honey, than honey from the comb.")

"She had shown considerable interest in reading at school, and I asked if she would be interested in reading directly from the Bible to me regularly. We would use her own Bible and examine a paragraph at a time.

"She became excited by the idea, ran into her bedroom to get her Bible, and what began as a father-daughter experiment in Bible reading has now become a family custom. We look forward to our reading, and I have often experienced a sense of God's presence and felt the Holy Spirit illuminate the passage as Sarah reads it. It's a form of meditation and it 'tastes good.' "

Pastor Fisher emphasized that simply reading and remembering God's words is not enough. Deuteronomy 6:7 says, "Impress them on your children. Talk about them when you sit at home and when you walk along the road, when you lie down and when you get up" (NIV).

The New Testament repeats this theme, admonishing us in Ephesians 6:4 to "bring them up in the training and instruction of the Lord" (NIV).

Unless we had to help raise a younger brother or sister, however, most of us had no experience raising children when we started with our own. When that begins to get to you, remember James 1:5: "If any of you lacks wisdom, he should ask God, who gives generously to all without finding fault, and it will be given to him" (NIV).

We know that probably a majority of even Christian parents would shock their children if they suddenly started having devotions alone, with the family, or with the individual children. But the verse above seems to say that we *can* start right where we are.

Christian singers and songwriters Bill and Gloria Gaither have always made it a practice to worship God in the everyday. They point out sunsets, flowers, animals, anything to their children that will spark a conversation about God and His creation and how His handiwork proves not only His greatness, but also His personal interest in all that He created— especially His children.

Other parents teach their children Scripture games, showing them how to pair off Bible characters like Jacob and Esau, Mary and Martha, Cain and Abel, and so forth. One developed an acrostic game where each letter in a child's first name was a reminder of a verse of Scripture he was to memorize. That way, the youngster soon memorized at least as many verses as there were letters in his first name.

Memorization is encouraged in Scripture, and many

church-related children's programs highlight this discipline. If you've never challenged your son or daughter to memorize Scripture, you'll be amazed at how much those tiny heads can retain. And even if they're too young to understand fully every word of every verse, the Scripture will stay with them until they mature and can figure them out for themselves. Of course, explaining verses as fully as they are able to comprehend helps them memorize all that much faster.

Psalms 78:5–7 says, "...He commanded our forefathers to teach their children, so the next generation would know them, even the children yet to be born, and they in turn would tell their children. Then they would put their trust in God . . ."(NIV).

Parents have an enormous responsibility. There will be days when this spiritual aspect alone will seem overwhelming to you. And there will be other days when you feel unspiritual, unqualified, unprepared. But you need to remember that your children are on loan from God. And while your energy, patience, and wisdom may be exhausted, the Father's never is. You may burn out, but the light of His inexhaustible power is always ours in Christ.

Creating a spiritual environment in the home begins with a Christ-committed husband and wife. Only then can we enlarge that circle of love and create a family rooted in Christian love and discipline. Developing in our children a loving, daily relationship with Christ requires skillful communication. Communication of biblical goals, and communication in general, is the subject of the next chapter.

Chapter Four

Communication: The Ear, Mouth, and Eye Gates

The atmosphere of the home inculcates Christian truth more effectively than the words we speak.
Howard G. Hendricks, *Say It With Love*

In Ephesians 6:4, the Apostle Paul uses the words *discipline* and *instruction* to describe God's method of raising children. We'll discuss discipline in detail in chapter six, but for the purposes of this chapter, it's important to understand that it means much more than correction. Richard Strauss calls it "charting a course for our children, guiding them along that course, and firmly but lovingly bringing them back to that course when they stray."

This assumes, of course, that you have established some goals for the raising of your children. If you haven't, prayerfully consider this basic list of biblical goals that we've established in our family:

1. Guide each of our children to salvation.
2. Show them by our example that they can know Jesus as their friend.
3. Give them the Bible to guide their lives.
4. Teach them, by our example, commitment to Christ and the Church.
5. Teach them spiritual obedience.

69

6. Show them the characteristics of Christian behavior such as righteousness, unselfishness, truthfulness.

It's important to have these goals firmly in mind when considering communication with children. The "what" of communication has to come before the "how." The children hear so much, see so much, and experience so much. How much of it is making an impact? We know that what they see us do is of more significance than what they hear us say, so if we are to instill in them our overall biblical precepts, those had better be clear in our minds and experienced in our hearts in advance. Howard Hendricks says that if your Christianity doesn't work at home, it doesn't work.

In the last chapter we discussed ways of making prayer, Bible reading and study, and Scripture memorization a vital part of our daily lives. So, now that we all have our acts together and are communing with God through prayer and Bible reading, meditating, and memorizing, we're ready to be super moms and dads and really communicate with our kids, right?

We don't mean to make it sound simple or like a gimmicky system that can't fail. The problem with this whole broad subject of communication with our kids is that we communicate one way or the other whether we intend to or not. If we say nothing to them, we are communicating volumes.

GLOW WORDS

Raising a child successfully sounds like a superhuman task. As a matter of fact, it is. It demands more than human resources have to offer. It requires supernatural wisdom and strength.

—Richard Strauss

You don't have to be a spiritual tower of power to begin instilling spiritual truth in your children, but the more you see how they emulate you, how they learn much more from what you do than from what you say, the more eager you'll find yourself to be an example of a spiritually alive Christian.

To communicate positive values, we have to take the initiative. We believe in openness, frankness, and even frequent—if not regular—family meetings. One of our rules is that anyone in the family can call a family meeting any time he feels one is needed. As soon as we can get everyone rounded up during a time that is free for each, we'll have a meeting. Sometimes one of the kids just wants to encourage everyone, so he'll request a meeting and read off a list of compliments and reasons why he appreciates the other members of the family. You can imagine how that warms us.

In chapter six we talk about things that need to be avoided and we're more specific about television, but limiting the viewing is one way we try to communicate to our kids that we want to be and will be different from people who do not love God. Unfortunately, we're finding that it also makes us different from many families, even in Christian school, who *do* love God, but who haven't seen the necessity to concentrate more on spiritual things and less on what the world has to offer.

We're not stick-in-the-mud weirdos about it, and we'll save the rest of that discussion for chapter six. Suffice it to say that as important as communicating is, *what* we communicate is paramount.

And don't think kids don't know the difference. One of ours came home recently with the announcement, "I'm glad I'm not in _____'s family. His mom never lets him do anything for himself or by himself. When he doesn't like something, he gets away with pouting all the time. And all he does is play with toys he saw on commercials on TV."

We were especially struck by the charge that the other parents never let the child do anything for himself. We always try to look for ways to help our children become independent. Jill sends them into the store for a loaf of bread or into the post office for stamps. They are expected to get the product and the change and hurry back to the car. Often, she says, they complain that it was difficult getting waited on because "No one would even look at me." People don't expect children to have responsibility.

We take our kids to restaurants and we have from day one. They learn how to act in public, and we insist that they obey. It's amazing how many kids today do not know the difference or decorum appropriate to family or public settings. We're not hesitant to remind the children that they are Christians and that our family is made up of ambassadors for Jesus Christ. A gentle reminder is usually all they need.

After thirty years of counseling parents and their children, Dr. Jay Kesler (former president of Youth For Christ/USA and now president of Taylor University) wrote in the April, 1985 issue of *Moody Monthly*, "I've found six principles that seem to ensure a family's success and well-being:

They openly communicate love.
They ensure an individual's personhood.
They clearly communicate rules and boundaries.
They confront problems openly and give them proper weight.
They are committed to the long-term.
They have Christ at the head.

Notice the prominence of communication?

One of our favorite stories is the traditional folk tale of an old man who had seven strong and sturdy sons.

One day the old man called the boys to him. Lying on his lap was a bundle of sticks tied together with cord.

"Which one of you is able to break the bundle of sticks?" the father asked.

The boys all were eager to prove their strength, but the youngest was the first to jump forward. He tried with all his might, but couldn't break the bundle.

In turn, each boy tried—and failed—to break the bundle of sticks. Finally, they came to the conclusion that it couldn't be done.

The father, however, said, "Bring the bundle here. I'll show you that it *can* be broken." He then took out a single stick and easily broke it. One by one he removed the sticks from the bundle, breaking each one, until all were broken.

"Sure, it's easy to do it that way," said one of the sons.

"Yes," said the old man, "and I want you to remember the lesson it teaches. If you split off from the family, you can easily be broken, and eventually the family can be broken up. But if we stick together, the family remains strong."

The Christian life is tough enough in this world ruled by Satan. Even a strong Christian from a good home can be deceived and misled if he tries to go it alone. That's why we fellowship with brothers and sisters in Christ, and that's why we stay in the Word and in prayerful communion with God. What strength can be imparted to individual Christian children when they know they are part of a family that plays together, prays together, and stays together!

Even young children can understand the strength that comes from communion with God. Karyn, at age six, was quite sensitive to spiritual things. One night while I was putting her to bed, she said, "Mommy, sometimes Satan comes into my mind and tells me to hate people that I love."

"What do you do?" I asked her.

"I pray and Jesus helps me love them."

"Why do you think he does that?"

"Because Satan is against God, and God is love," Karyn replied.

We've talked about the importance of communicating our values to our children both by example and by instruction, but there is another essential element in communication—listening. Listening is more important than talking because it is a self-giving activity. It is conscious attention. It communicates love and concern.

Sometimes we tend to think we know the answer to everyone else's problems—and what the problems are—even before they get them out of their mouths. This is especially true for parents.

Our memories go back to before our children were born. How could they possibly encounter anything new, anything we don't already know about?

They share their struggle, their frustration has burst forth, half-baked, not even well-articulated. Yet before you know it, Wonderparent is pontificating on (1) why it's not really a problem to start with and (2) the logical way to solve it. Boom! Parent gets minus-one.

Be quiet and listen. And when you've heard it all, keep quiet. Sometimes a child works up the courage to share a problem, and that's all he wanted. He didn't ask for advice. No, it's not implied in his sharing that he's also asking for our input. He wants an ear. He wants an eye. He wants attention, undivided, no eyes darting about as we mentally choreograph our solution.

Nod, wince, grimace, scowl in sympathy, but don't say anything. Make the child ask or in some other way indicate an openness to advice. If it doesn't come, you might just say, "Wow, I can imagine how that must make you feel. You're frustrated, aren't you?"

Or, "I can tell that upsets you. I'd be upset too. In fact, I'm upset for you, and I'll be praying that you'll find the right solution. Is there anything else I can do in the meantime?"

You may be surprised that what the child wants at that point is concrete action. "Could you call so-and-so for me?" or "Could you help me write a letter?" or "Could I get an advance on next week's allowance so . . .?"

If you're asked for advice, you might still want to bite your tongue for a few minutes. Perhaps their problem *is* old hat and you *did* go through it when you were their age. Still, it's not simple and advice shouldn't come too quickly. The place to start is in identifying with them. Kids always seem impressed when they find that we have been through a similar experience, but that can be shot through too if we prove we have forgotten how troubling it was.

In his book *The Family That Listens* (Victor Books, 1978),

Dr. H. Norman Wright warns against stereotyping children. "If you feel your child is a complainer, a whiner, a bully, or procrastinator, it may affect what you think he is saying. If we think, 'Oh, he's a whiner, it's not important what he says,' we may miss learning some vital information."

It's been said that we have the capacity to listen at five times the speed anyone can talk. That's why it's hard work to maintain eye contact and not start picking through our mental card files for the answer before we've heard the question.

Quiet, patient listening is a skill that can take years to learn. Rare is the parent who is simply made that way. The earlier we begin practicing, the better we'll be by the time the deep adolescent discussions roll around.

GLOW WORDS

Don't threaten—you decimate your own authority.

Don't bribe—bargaining usually makes you the loser.

Don't lose your temper—a clear demonstration of lack of control.

Don't refuse to explain—they'll go elsewhere and you're on the outside.

Don't use sarcasm or embarrassment—the fastest way to demolish a relationship.

Don't dash their dreams—your ticket into the generation gap.

—Howard Hendricks, *Heaven Help the Home!*

Sometimes it takes a formal family powwow to get important ideas out to everyone or to solve a problem that is affecting everyone. Such meetings also teach social behavior, order, and "public speaking." The only way to have an effective, all-family meeting is to be sure it's held at a time when everyone can be there. Generally, that means around a mealtime, most likely dinner. Every member of the family should have an equal voice, including the youngest children, providing they can talk. If you have an infant who can only babble, it can be fun to pretend to give him the floor and let everyone laugh and clap when he tries to say something. As long as it's clear to everyone that you're not poking fun at him, everybody enjoys it, including the baby, who eats up the attention.

Let everyone know at the beginning what it is you're trying to accomplish with the meeting. Is it just to let everyone have his say, or are you trying to reassign chores, decide on where to vacation next summer, or deal with a discipline problem or some unresolved argument?

We try to include the B-E-S-T principles even in our family meetings. When someone says something, we might ask if what was said was Blessing, Edifying, or just Sharing. All our kids are good at sharing, even if it's just an "I like my school," which we always hear from Andrea. The tiny ones love it, even though they have little idea what's going on.

Sometimes we'll call a meeting just to keep the lines of communication open. It might not be terribly structured. In fact, we might have one on the spur of the moment, just before it's time to clear the table. I might say, "Let's have a meeting. Jim, tell us what's going on in your life. Is there anything we could be doing to help you more, or something we could be doing better as parents or brothers or sisters?"

Sometimes we'll even play charades at a family meeting. With the age span of our kids, we're talking about very obvious charades. Jill might be down on all fours with Karyn on her back to signify Mary on her way to Bethlehem. We always want to teach something, even if we're just having fun.

We divide up the chores in a way Jill thought of a few years ago. She had assigned tasks to everyone—like loading or unloading the top or bottom of the dishwasher, setting the table, getting the paper, putting out the vitamins, and so on. But at one family meeting the kids complained because they got tired of the same chores after several weeks. Jill's stroke of genius was to write the chores on popsicle sticks to be drawn each week. You can never draw the same chore two weeks in a row. Even if you draw a chore you hate, it's only for a week.

We always try to end our family meetings on a high note with a snack or a game.

What we're trying to communicate is a sense of community. The family is not parents versus kids or some of the children versus some of the others. Kids will squabble and bicker and fight occasionally, and mom and dad will find themselves grouchy or irritable, but with the right ingredients in the everyday mix—like family meetings and private heart-to-heart talks—every member of the family will get the message: This is a place where we can all participate, belong, and feel needed. This is a place where we try to put into practice the elements of 1 Corinthians 13 love.

So, have your "summits." A private one with God regularly. A high summit with your mate to talk about anything and everything, family related or not. And a family summit where you handle the four Ds: decisions, duties, dingleberries (gripe sessions), and development (something to learn).

Communication is a two-way street that involves listening and paying attention, being quiet or giving advice only when asked, and remembering that by being remote and not inter-acting, we are communicating more than we want to.

Affirmation, building self-esteem in a child so he is truly prepared to meet the cold, cruel world, is also a matter of com-munication. This very specific, positive kind of communica-tion, which we'll discuss in the next chapter, is calculated to have an immediate and a long-range benefit for each child.

Chapter Five

Affirm a Foundation

The elements of self-esteem are belonging, worth, and confidence. Belonging comes from our relationships at home; worth comes from what we are intrinsically—made in the image of God; confidence comes from what we can do. Recognize and affirm a child for who he is and praise him for what he does.

—J. Allan Petersen

We could write a whole other book about *affirmation*. Lots of people have (and we've read them all—at least it seems that way). Yet, there's a reason so much has been written recently on this subject. The experts, both Christian and secular, have come to the realization that if there has been one area of neglect in this business of raising children it is affirmation.

Affirmation is the process of building a child's feeling of self-worth. Dorothy Briggs, in *Your Child's Self-Esteem: The Key to His Life* (Doubleday, 1970), writes, "What's the greatest gift you can give to your child? Help him to like himself."

There are various components to affirmation: acceptance, unconditional loving, praise, encouragement, self-esteem, touching. We're going to discuss each of these in turn. To affirm a child, we must first make him feel accepted. Long before he can really understand the process, a child must be loved unconditionally. Praise and encouragement bolster the feelings of self-esteem that result. Touching, the fourth and most important element in Dr. Ed Wheat's B-E-S-T acronym, brings it all home in a tactile way.

Jill clipped this charming little anecdote by Laura C. Patterson from *Woman's Day* (March 8, 1983). It wonderfully demonstrates the family-wide acceptance that we are trying to create in our 1 Corinthians 13 family.

> Many years ago, when my little girl had a nasty case of chicken pox, she called from her room in a moment of feeling down and lonely, "Who loves me?"
> The whole family answered instantly and in unison: "We do!"
> She continued to ask often and was always so delighted with the reply, she kept it up long after her recovery.
> Some years later, while doing what seemed to be an endless load of dishes, I impulsively tried out my daughter's question for myself. The replies were quick, cheerful, and resounding. Suddenly the dishes no longer seemed so terrible.
> I was not too surprised when in the midst of studying for exams, my husband took his turn at asking. He too received the usual reply and seemed to study more easily afterward.
> So started our tradition of sorts. No matter which of us asks and no matter when we ask, the answer is always there. If we are overburdened, worried, tired, or sad, it never fails to cure what ails us. It's like a pat on the back or a hug—those voices ringing out love all over the house.

Acceptance

We're enthusiastic, unabashed, unapologetic James Dobson devotees, as are most Christian parents who've been exposed to his ministry. We've read every word of every one of his best-selling books (at least once and frequently more than once) and his ministry magazine, and we both listen to him on the radio every day.

In the opening chapter of his *Hide or Seek* (Revell, 1979) he tells a dramatic, true story that—while depressing—best illustrates, by negative example, the absolute necessity for acceptance in a child's life. See if you don't agree.

> He began his life with all the classic handicaps and disadvantages. His mother was a powerfully built, dominating

woman who found it difficult to love anyone. She had been married three times, and her second husband divorced her because she beat him up regularly. The father of the child I'm describing was her third husband; he died of a heart attack a few months before the child's birth. As a consequence, the mother had to work long hours from his earliest childhood.

She gave him no affection, no love, no discipline, and no training during those early years. She even forbade him to call her at work. Other children had little to do with him, so he was alone most of the time. He was absolutely rejected from his earliest childhood. He was ugly and poor and untrained and unlovable. When he was thirteen years old a school psychologist commented that he probably didn't even know the meaning of the word "love." During adolescence, the girls would have nothing to do with him and he fought with the boys.

Despite a high IQ, he failed academically, and finally dropped out during his third year of high school. He thought he might find a new acceptance in the Marine Corps; they reportedly built men, and he wanted to be one. But his problems went with him. The other marines laughed at him and ridiculed him. He fought back, resisted authority, and was court-martialed and thrown out of the marines with an undesirable discharge.

So there he was—a young man in his early twenties—absolutely friendless and shipwrecked. He was small and scrawny in stature. He had an adolescent squeak in his voice. He was balding. He had no talent, no skill, no sense of worthiness. He didn't even have a driver's license. Once again he thought he could run from his problems, so he went to live in a foreign country. But he was rejected there too. Nothing had changed.

While there, he married a girl who herself had been an illegitimate child. He brought her back to America with him. Soon, she began to develop the same contempt for him that everyone else displayed. She bore him two children, but he never enjoyed the status and respect that a father should have.

His marriage continued to crumble. His wife demanded more and more things that he could not provide. Instead of being his ally against the bitter world, as he hoped, she became his most vicious opponent. She could outfight him, and she learned to bully him. On one occasion, she locked him in the bathroom as punishment. Finally, she forced him to leave.

He tried to make it on his own, but he was terribly lonely. After days of solitude, he went home and literally begged her to take him back. He surrendered all pride. He crawled. He accepted humiliation. He came on her terms. Despite his meager salary, he brought her seventy-eight dollars as a gift, asking her to take it and spend it any way she wished.

But she laughed at him. She belittled his feeble attempts to supply the family's needs. She ridiculed his failure. She made fun of his sexual impotency in front of a friend. At one point he fell on his knees and wept bitterly, as the greater darkness of his private nightmare enveloped him.

Finally, in silence, he pleaded no more. No one wanted him. No one had ever wanted him. He was perhaps the most rejected man of our time. His ego lay shattered in fragmented dust. The next day he was a strangely different man. He arose, went to the garage, and took down a rifle he had hidden there. He carried it with him to his newly acquired job at a book-storage building.

And from a window on the third floor of that building, shortly after noon, November 22, 1963, he sent two bullets crashing into the head of President John Fitzgerald Kennedy.

What a sad, sad story. Lee Harvey Oswald had not one of the elements of affirmation we'll talk about in this chapter.

GLOW WORDS

Children need:
A sense of significance
Security
Acceptance
Love
Praise
Discipline
God.

—John M. Drescher
Seven Things Children Need

John M. Drescher, in his book *Seven Things Children Need*, (Herald Press, 1976), lists several factors causing a child to feel a lack of acceptance:

> First, constantly criticizing a child creates feelings of failure, rejection, and inadequacy.
>
> Second, comparing a child with others shows a lack of acceptance. . . . Continual comparison builds inferiority feelings which harm personality development.
>
> Third, expecting a child to achieve his parents' unfulfilled dreams causes him to feel unaccepted.
>
> Fourth, overprotecting a child often contributes to his feeling of unacceptance. . . . By overprotecting the child, the spirit of adventure can be damaged, instilling a spirit of fear rather than faith.
>
> Fifth, expecting too much of a child builds feelings of unacceptance. A child can sense even the unspoken anxiousness of a parent that he be a model child.

Jill and I are constantly on guard lest any of these negative patterns creep into our family life. There is one in particular that we'd like to talk about from our own experience—expecting your children to fulfill your own dreams.

I guess you'd say I was a better-than-average all-around athlete, but my best sport was baseball. I caught for Wake Forest University and began my professional career in the Philadelphia Phillies minor-league system. I worked hard to become a big-league ballplayer, but it wasn't meant to be. I had to adapt to the disappointment and ultimately I used the skills developed in promoting athletic events at Wake Forest to land a job in the Phillies front office. From there I went on to the presidency of a minor-league baseball team in Spartanburg, South Carolina, to become general manager of the Chicago Bulls, then the Atlanta Hawks, and then the 76ers. Despite it all, I'm still aware, deep down inside, that a big-league ballplayer was sidetracked years ago.

But now that Jim, still a preteen, is such a good baseball player that he is sought by Little League coaches in different towns, I have to be careful not to start reliving my own dream through Jim. Even though Jim loves the game and may himself dream of becoming a big leaguer, his dream has to be his own, and his ultimate achievement or disappointment must be his own as well. If he were to make the big leagues one day, we would share his joy, of course. And if that's his dream and he doesn't make it, we would support him in his disappointment. But what a burden it would be if he felt he had to be the big leaguer his father never was! How doubly disappointing to miss a goal if you're striving for it not just for yourself but for your father as well.

What Pat has been talking about with regard to the boys is true for me with our daughters too. I adjusted quickly to finishing first runner-up to Miss Illinois in 1972, even knowing that many people thought I could have gone on to win Miss America. My peace about where I finished had come from being open to whatever God had in store for me, whether I finished first or second.

But as Karyn and Andrea and Sarah grow up and show promise of beauty and musical talent, the temptation might be there—not to make up for any short-circuited aspirations of mine, but just because "they're our daughters and who else could be Miss America?" We'll have to be sure of our motives before encouraging (not pushing) them toward similar competition.

We, as parents, must consciously find ways to let our children know they are accepted. The seven guidelines discussed below come from John Drescher and are accompanied by some of the ways we try to implement them.

1. *Recognize the child as unique.*

We always try to call our kids by their own names. We don't say that our number one son or number two son did this or that or that one of our Korean daughters said something cute. We use their names, introduce them by their names, and maintain their individuality. One of Jill's pet peeves is when someone makes a remark to us about our children in front of them without speaking directly to them.

Individuality also comes up in the area of discipline, which we cover in the next chapter. When our children remind her that she's not being fair with them, Jill reminds them that life isn't fair. But, more to the point, they're all different. Some of the children don't respond to certain types of discipline the way others do, so she has to decide what's best.

2. *Help the child find satisfaction in achievements.*

In standing by, rather than being overprotective, we not only accept the child, but also prepare him for life.

Expecting too little of a child can demonstrate a lack of faith on your part. Even limited kids have reachable goals.

3. *Let the child know you love him, want him, and really enjoy him.*

Remember, "Children are a gift of the Lord . . ." (Psalms 127:3 NAS).

A child senses quickly the nature of the parent's feelings toward him. Jill has always felt that every child needs at least one adult who he knows is crazy about him.

John Drescher adds, "Happy is the child who is continually reminded by his parents that they want him and enjoy him to the fullest. How does a child know? He knows it when the parent takes time to be with him, to help him with his little projects, and when the parent takes every opportunity to demonstrate love for him."

4. *Accept the child's friends. Home should be a place where he can freely bring his friends, and a place where his friends love to come.*

We feel it's important to establish an atmosphere like this before the kids get into high school. If they bring their friends to our home, we won't have to worry about whom they're with, where they are, and what they're up to.

5. *Maintain an honest, genuine relationship with the child.*

We should admit our own mistakes and shortcomings, admit the fact that we were not perfect children and that we are not perfect parents. Rather than ridiculing a child for a childish fear or hesitancy, we should assure him that we felt the same way when we were little.

6. *Listen to what the child is saying.*

Love, for a child, is usually spelled T-I-M-E. (More on listening in chapter four, and more on time in chapter two).

7. *Treat the child as a person of worth.*

This goes along with our counsel about treating children as guests in your own home, using good manners, politely saying please and thank you and excuse me. One thing that saddens us is to hear the way some moms and dads speak to their children in the grocery store or mall — public places. We can only imagine what it must be like in the privacy of their homes! Children have a remarkable ability to live up to their reputations, good or bad.

"Acceptance," says author Drescher, "means respecting a child's feelings and his personality while letting him know that wrong behavior is unacceptable. Acceptance means that parents *like* the child all the time, regardless of his acts or ideas."

There's a story we heard a few years ago that is a heartbreaking reminder of our need for unconditional love. It goes like this.

> One night toward the end of the Vietnam war, a son called his parents after months of silence. His mother was surprised and overjoyed to learn he was on his way home.
>
> "Mom," he said, "would it be okay if I brought a buddy home with me? He got hurt pretty bad, and he has only one eye, one arm, and one leg."
>
> "Sure, son," she replied. "He sounds like a brave man. We can find room for him for a while."
>
> "But, Mom, he may have to live with us—he doesn't have any other place to go."
>
> "Well, all right," she relented. "We could try it for six months or so."
>
> "No, Mom. He's as close to me as my own flesh and blood. He needs us. He's only got one arm, one leg, and one eye. He's really in bad shape."
>
> The mother lost patience. "Son, you're being pretty unrealistic. I know you've been through a lot in the war. But that boy will be a drag on you and a problem for all of us. Be reasonable."

Suddenly, the phone clicked dead. The next day the parents received a telegram informing them that their son had leapt to his death from his tenth-floor room the night before. A week later, they received the casket and looked down with unspeakable sadness at the body of their one-eyed, one-armed, one-legged son.

Unconditional Love

Real love is unconditional. That is the kind of love Christ has for each of us, and each parent should try to have for his children.

Louis Evans, Jr., says it well in *Bold Commitment* (Victor Books, 1983):

> [God] never turns away from us, His children, just because we disappoint Him. He comes back to us again and again, often with honest encounter, but always with untiring covenant love. As I see it, the epitome of this love is Jesus, who was God's act of love toward a hostile world. Nothing could drive Him from His covenant; His commitment was firm. No degree of inconvenience and no broken agreements could suppress the flow of His love.
>
> A covenant says, "My commitment is to you as a person, not to the roles you fulfill for my need or satisfaction. There is nothing you can say or do that will ever make me stop loving you."
>
> All of us yearn for this kind of bold commitment from the human being most important to us. Without it, we just never become the people we were meant to be.

Isn't that the goal for parental love?

Of course, we, as finite humans, don't have the capacity for truly unconditional love. We are fallen creatures and many conditions get in the way of our true love. That's why it's only possible to love our mates or our children unconditionally if we get out of the way and let God do the loving.

Dr. Ross Campbell, in his book *How to Really Love Your Child* (Victor Books, 1977) defines unconditional love in the parent-child relationship as loving the child, "no matter what."

No matter what he looks like. No matter what he does. No matter what his shortcomings. "This does not mean, of course, that we always like his behavior. Unconditional love means we love the *child* even when at times we may detest his *behavior*."

Scientific research has clearly shown that adults who as infants felt deeply and constantly loved by their parents tend to be happy in their romances. But babies who are loved inconsistently, or insufficiently, are more likely in later life to follow one of two quite different patterns: They may either cling too much or be unable to make close attachments. Children who receive love are more able to give—and accept—it.

Dr. Campbell says he must constantly remind himself that the objects of his unconditional love are children. They will act like children. Much of childish behavior is unpleasant; if he does his part and loves them in spite of it, they will be able to mature and give up childish ways. And if he loves them only when they please him (conditional love), they will not feel genuinely loved but will feel insecure and lose self-esteem.

Children hear us when we say we love them, but they believe us when we prove it. Recently I asked Karyn, "How do you know I love you?"

She answered very matter-of-factly. "Because you always tell me, Daddy."

But what if I only said it and never proved it? Would she *know* I loved her? If Jill and I want our children to know how we feel about them, that we love them, we need to do more than tell them. We need to *act* as though we love them.

We like this love acronym:

L—Listen.

O—Overlook faults.

V—Value opinions.

E—Express yourself openly, avoiding pouting, guessing games, silent treatments, and hints.

"Dear children, let us not love with words or tongue but with actions and in truth" (1 John 3:18 NIV).

GLOW WORDS

If a child lives with criticism, he learns to condemn;

If a child lives with hostility, he learns to fight;

If a child lives with ridicule, he learns to be shy;

If a child lives with shame, he learns to feel guilty.

If a child lives with tolerance, he learns to be patient;

If a child lives with encouragement, he learns confidence;

If a child lives with praise, he learns to appreciate;

If a child lives with fairness, he learns justice;

If a child lives with security, he learns to have faith;

If a child lives with approval, he learns to like himself;

If a child lives with acceptance and friendship, he learns to find love in the world.

—Dorothy Law Nolte

Praise

According to J. Allan Petersen, studies have shown that for every negative thing you say to a child, you must say four positive things just to keep the balance. "When you realize how quick parents are to nitpick, to criticize, and how slow we are to praise, you realize that overpraising is hardly a danger."

This is a strange, elusive element in affirming a child because praise can be misused. It's a little like chocolate syrup. Even the worst chocoholic would be turned off by an entire can of syrup with a marble-sized scoop of ice cream floating in it. There's a temptation, once we see a child's eyes light up after we've praised him, to lay it on thick.

Tell a child every day that he's the greatest kid in the world and he may just catch on to you. You may temporarily bolster sagging spirits, and you may convince him that *you* think he's special. But what happens when you want to sincerely compliment him for something?

Perhaps he's drawn a nice picture, or colored something and stayed within the lines. Or maybe he has written a typical paper for a child his age, but his handwriting is exceptional. Rather than gushing over his creation and trying to convince him he's the next Ernest Hemingway, be specific and be temperate. "I enjoyed that part about the bears in your story a lot. And your handwriting is better than ever."

Has your child ever asked you something like "If I wasn't your kid, would you still think I was the best player on the team?" They want the truth. They don't want overblown superlatives.

There's nothing wrong with telling a child he's your favorite eight-year-old in the whole world. Of course, if you tell him he's your favorite kid, he may do a double take and ask about his brother or sister.

We affirm our adopted daughters by telling them how special they are to us and how we chose them, so we got a kick out of reading a story about a set of parents who adopted three children. They told them from the earliest moments that they had selected them to join the family; the children were their choice. Later they heard the children boasting to their friends, "Our parents chose us; they didn't *have* to take us."

Encouragement

This is an investment. It costs so little and reaps such benefits! Identifying with a child encourages him. Doing something practical with him or for him encourages him. This is real skill training. Anything that increases self-mastery or control of his environment—from tying shoestrings to doing calculus. How many tears over frustrating chores would be eliminated if we just shared the task with the child the first few times? They learn, they watch, they catch on. And finally they can do it themselves with confidence.

Telling a child that you love him, even when he's ornery, can be encouraging, even if he won't admit it. That line will usually elicit a smile, however. "Nothing you can do will make me stop loving you. Even if you scowl all day and act icky. I still love you." It's hard for any kid to stand up to that kind of unconditional love-motivated encouragement.

The most natural way to encourage is to notice. Notice what? Notice everything. Look for things your child does right. Catch him in the act of being good, doing good, acting kind. Be appreciative!

"I'm glad you're my daughter." Try that line on a pouting girl. First she'll want to know why. Be ready with a long list of things you admire about her. Be serious and be sincere. You shouldn't have to make up anything. We have a little game where one person — most often Mom or Dad — says with a sly smile, I know something good about_____," inserting one child's name. Everyone asks, "What?" And then we proceed to tell it.

One of the most encouraging things you can do for a child is to give him attention. For no reason. Maybe you're passing each other in the house, as you've done a dozen times a day for years. Reach out and smack him on the arm, tousle his hair, tickle him, make a funny face or noise, try to get a smile or a laugh. You're doing something just for him, something that says, "You're here and you're somebody, and to me you're special. You're worth the effort to communicate with."

Dr. Kay Kuzma sees lack of attention as the source of many behavior problems: "Without attention, children don't feel loved. So if their love cups are empty, they try to get them filled with attention. They seek approval, they show off, they try to be good. But how often do good children get much attention? Not often.

"Most unloved children find they get more attention by being bad. Getting attention becomes such an overwhelming need that these children cease to care if it is positive or negative."

To encourage Jimmy, Pat arranged to take him and five other pitchers on his Little League team to see Claude Osteen, pitching coach of the Philadelphia Phillies. Interesting to Pat was that Osteen, besides giving the kids a lot of pointers, wanted to talk of little else but his own sons who are high school and collegiate pitchers.

During the visit to Veterans Stadium, Pat introduced every player by name to Osteen and to several other Phillies and officials. One of the other fathers who went along said, "I don't believe it. You know everybody by name."

Learning people's names happens to be one of Pat's gifts, a trick from the old Dale Carnegie course, but in this case it was all part of the package designed to encourage his own son.

Also encouraging to any child is the realization that he can be wrong, can make mistakes, can even disagree with us without "blowing it." That he or she will be accepted for differences as well as agreement gives an essential feeling of security to a child. Colleen Townsend Evans, writing in the March/April, 1984, issue of *Today's Christian Woman,* commented, "A family is where the umbrella of love is so strong and so broad that differences can be allowed. Part of respecting one another is allowing people to be the persons God created them to be."

This whole idea of affirmation was controversial until a few years ago, because most parents were afraid of raising cocky, self-absorbed kids who would think they were the center of the universe. Of course, no one wants to do that, and it *is* a danger in praising, encouraging, and worrying about your child's self-esteem.

But consider the alternative. Would you rather raise a child who leaves your home at eighteen thinking he's the center of the universe and—if nothing else—loved unconditionally, or who thinks he's unworthy, unloved, and is emotionally bankrupt?

Perhaps at eighteen conceit is not much better than a feeling of worthlessness, but the future is much brighter for the former. Yes, he will come crashing down when not everyone at college or in the marketplace thinks he's so wonderful or hangs on his every word. He'll be disappointed when his work is not praised the way it was at home.

But he'll mature, he'll grow up, he'll start thinking of others. He'll be sensitive and will likely be an encourager. He'll know he has a bedrock of love and acceptance and esteem at home, and down deep he'll believe he's worthy of that, no matter what anyone else says. These are the children who love to come home and enjoy giving back the attention and warmth they received when they lived there.

The hopelessly defeated person, however, will hardly ever be convinced of his worth. No matter what success or luck comes his way, no matter if people think his looks or his ideas or his talents are wonderful, he'll believe what was programmed into his mind at home: low self-worth, low self-esteem, low value.

We were once asked, as a family, to handle the chapel service at the kids' school, Bethel Baptist Christian in Cherry Hill, New Jersey. Bob, Karyn, and Jill sang together and Karyn and Jill also sang solos. I delivered the message.

Jimmy, who isn't comfortable singing in front of people, asked if he could run the sound system for us. He had never done it alone before, but we were pleased that he asked. With a little coaching beforehand, he was conscientious and confident and handled everything perfectly and professionally.

Even though he didn't sing with us, we know he felt involved and important, and he gained a sense of accomplishment. Jill plans to take him with her on her singing engagements whenever possible.

Self-Esteem

Self-esteem, according to Dr. Jim Dobson, is that sense of personal worth that provides our children with the inner strength they will need to survive the obstacles they will face while growing up. Drawn here from his book *Hide or Seek* are these seven strategies by which we can instill confidence and self-worth in our boys and girls.

1. *Examine your own values.* What if your children are ordinary? Is that all right with you? What if they are not the best in anything they do? In fact, what if they are below average, even—perish the thought—homely? Children can tell the difference between being loved and being held in high esteem. What impression are you conveying to them?

2. *Teach a "no-knock" policy.* Allow no self-criticism. People who feel inferior tend to make it known frequently. They believe their own bad press.

3. *Help your child to compensate.* An individual counterbalances weaknesses by capitalizing on his strengths. He must be able to say, "I may not be the most popular student in school, but I'm the best trumpet player in the band!"

4. *Help your child to compete.* Even though we know that the world values beauty, brains, and brawn, and we believe and teach the true values of life—love for mankind, integrity, truthfulness, and devotion to God—we should help our children where we can. If their teeth are crooked and we can afford braces, we should get them. If they need a tutor, provide one. Can we help them look their best? We are allies in a fight for survival.

5. *Discipline without damaging self-esteem.* Belief in spanking is no excuse for taking out your frustrations on your child. It offers no license to punish him in front of others or treat him with disrespect.

6. *Keep a close eye on the classroom.* Make sure your child reaches the typical milestones at the right time, for instance, that he knows how to read at the end of second grade. Tutors, changes of schools, classes, or teachers can sometimes be of value. Slow learner? De-emphasize academic achievement if necessary. Dr. Dobson says, "You would not demand that a

crippled child become a track star, yet too many parents want their 'average students' to become Rhodes Scholars."

7. *Avoid overprotection and dependency.* Each year a child should make more of his own decisions. A seven-year-old, for example, is usually capable of selecting his own clothing for the day. He should be keeping his room straightened and making his bed.

In our home, everyone has jobs. I'm a mom who feels it's a great disservice to a child to do something for him that he can do himself. For instance, every morning the children are assigned to get their lunch beverage into the thermos, select the right sandwich from the refrigerator (made by Pat the night before), make their selection of healthy snacks to add to their lunch (from sugar-free cookies, fruit bars, granola, and fruit), and enclose a napkin. When they get home, they are expected to clean their lunch boxes.

Each chooses what to wear (within reason and with some overruling by Mom when necessary). They are also expected to do their assigned chores without being told, put all important school papers on the bulletin board for Mom to see, and keep me informed as to when they need fees and dues. Even the four-year-old is expected to keep me up-to-date.

Dr. Dobson concludes: "These are the ways to teach a child to appreciate his genuine significance, regardless of the shape of his nose or the size of his ears or the efficiency of his mind. *Every* child is entitled to hold up his head in confidence and security."

Touching

Perhaps the most direct way to affirm is to touch. Touching says, "You are acceptable."

As we've made clear, we're into touching. At first it just seemed like a good idea. Good for the psyche. But the more we study it, the more indispensable it seems.

The skin is the largest organ of the human body and researchers say that it has a built-in need to be touched and stimulated. Again, here we're dealing with parent-child touching, though this nonsexual need exists in adults too.

Experts believe that children who are touched regularly and lovingly actually mature faster physically. Experiments with sick or orphaned babies have shown that with loving caresses on a regular basis, they quickly catch up to their normal peers in physical size.

On the negative side, according to Ashley Montagu, research has shown that many adult neurotics, depression victims, prostitutes, and outcasts give evidence of "skin hunger," a lack in their childhood of human physical contact other than punishment.

Pediatricians are now recommending giving babies massages and back rubs daily, just for their physical and psychological well-being. We have done this more with baby Michael than we did with the older kids when they were babies because we simply didn't know about it then. We're making up for lost time with the others, however! As they grow up, other forms of touching affirmation may be used.

Jill will always stay with our kids if they are in the hospital, never allowing them to be tied to a bed. She even held Bobby all night when he was going in for tests as an infant and was not allowed to be fed. He cried all night in her arms, but she would not leave him. Four out of our six have been hospitalized for periods of time and with each one, Jill was there around the clock.

Besides the obvious physical—even medical—need to be touched, the psychological need seems to us to be just as strong. A gentle, caring, loving touch means so many things to a person. Even kids going through stages where they don't think they want to be hugged or get back rubs should be encouraged to submit anyway. Loving, parental hands can win them over, and in spite of the protest, they'll enjoy long-range benefits.

There are studies showing that teens who have sexual problems or "have to get married" often have histories of too little physical contact in their immediate families. The young people may be compensating for cuddling that should have continued into adolescence but which ended by the time they were twelve.

Have you ever had trouble getting your child to understand your point of view or getting him to see that you have his best interest at heart? Move close. Get an arm around him. Gently massage his neck. The anger, the resentment, the orneriness often will melt away. When Jill taught elementary school, she learned the value of touching a child. If one had difficulty remembering how to spell a word or recite a verse or figure a math problem, a gentle touch from Jill would often make the difficulty disappear.

Friends of ours had a child who went through a brief but troublesome period of stuttering. The toddler's face turned red as he worked to make the words come out. The parents were advised to simply touch his shoulder and gaze into his eyes as if they had all the time in the world and that there was nothing more important than patiently listening to him. The problem of two to three weeks duration disappeared in a couple of days.

An arm around the shoulder, the drawing close of a loved one, says more than words can ever say. Dr. Ed Wheat says it's paramount in a marriage, and we say it's a major, crucial, irreplaceable child-rearing tool.

Don't raise a child without it.

Nothing is more gratifying than to see your children pick up on your example of affirmation. More than a year ago, Pat came home with gifts for the children. He gave Jim a Phillies' yearbook and Bob a leather wallet.

From the beginning it was clear that Jim was jealous and much more interested in his little brother's wallet than in the yearbook. The latter was discarded within a few days.

Recently, at a picnic, we celebrated Jim's birthday. From Bob he received a handmade card with a drawing of Jim hitting a home run and a message assuring him that Bob loved him. And, personally wrapped, was Bob's leather wallet. "I remembered that you liked it so much."

Bob has surprised us in other ways. As a third grader he tried out for the school play, *Martin the Cobbler*. He won the lead part and asked if Jill would help him learn it. It was three pages of script. They went over it once, and he never asked again.

Every few days, Jill asked him if he needed any more help. No, he said. Was he learning it? Yes. She trusted him, patted him on the back in affirmation and let him go on his own.

When the big day came, he looked darling in gray hair, wire-rim glasses, big boots, standing before the crowd, working on shoes. The whole play went perfectly. He knew every line and delivered each with confidence, no nervousness, no hesitation. He was secure and comfortable. We believe that the strokes and the love Bob and all our kids get at home enable them to perform in public.

There are many ways to affirm a child, and we've discussed some of them. "Conveying love to a child," according to Dr. Ross Campbell, "can be broadly classified into four areas: eye contact, physical contact, focused attention, and discipline." This last area—discipline—is a large topic and the next chapter will be devoted entirely to it.

Chapter Six

Discipline:
Have a Spare Rod?

> Obedience to father and mother is the first step in enabling the child to learn self-control and the ability to live constructively outside of his home. Ultimately this can lead to submission and obedience to God.
> —Ella May Miller, *I Am a Mother*

Welcome to the most controversial child-rearing subject anywhere. Let us start by quickly positioning ourselves so you'll know whether to (1) keep reading and nod at our brilliant insights, (2) toss the book in the trash, (3) write us a nasty letter, or (4) use the book as a paddle with which to spank your child.

We agree with those who say that there is a big difference between discipline and punishment, and that rarely, if ever, is true punishment required. This is not to say that discipline-oriented spankings aren't required. They are, and we'll discuss that a little later.

Some parents think that discipline is the same thing as punishment. But *discipline* comes from a Latin word meaning "to teach." Good discipline teaches. It is our responsibility as parents to guide our children toward the self-discipline that is essential to maturity.

In *Dare to Discipline* (Tyndale, 1973), Dr. James Dobson

writes, "It should come as no surprise that our beloved children have hangups; we have sacrificed this generation on the altar of overindulgence, permissiveness, and smother-love. Certainly, other factors have contributed to the present unsettled youth scene, but I believe the major cause has been related to the anarchy that existed in millions of American homes."

But things are changing. Dr. Howard Hendricks in his *Heaven Help the Home!* (Victor Books, 1973), advises parents not to be afraid to say no. Many of the parents he counseled confessed they were afraid to carry out what they knew was best for the child. Dr. Hendricks asked, "Afraid? Of what?"

"I feared my child would turn against me, that he would think I didn't love him."

Dr. Hendricks says, "You will seldom lose a child by doing the right thing for him. Intelligent, scriptural love is always unconditional. If you love your child, you will discipline him. If you do not discipline him, you do not really love him. Your primary concern is not what he thinks of you now, but what he will think twenty years from now."

Author Skip Ross, in his *Say Yes to Your Potential* (Word, 1985), writes: "I believe the parents of this generation of young people have experienced some of the disastrous results of their own permissive upbringing and the pendulum is beginning to swing back to raising children in a tradition of respect for elders, respect for rules, and respect for themselves.

"There are hundreds of thousands of young people across our nation today, looking for someone who loves them enough to say, 'This is the way, walk in it.' It's not an attitude that approaches with the clenched fist of demand, but with the open hand of love which reaches out to say, "Come on, follow me. I'll show you the way."

Dr. Hendricks also reminds parents that discipline is a long-range process. "Allow your children the luxury of a few mistakes. There is something worse—not making mistakes and arresting growth. Maturity comes with responsibility."

We've always believed that tremendous emotional security

comes from consistent discipline. We're close to our kids. We didn't let them cry a lot as infants. We let them sleep with us occasionally when they were tiny. But we're no less tough on them when we need to be.

Bedtime is absolute, though Jill is a little more resolute than I am about that. The TV is regulated. We don't eat candy in our family. Jill learned as a teacher that the best route is to start out tough and loosen up as the year progresses and as you see that the kids can handle increased responsibility.

One of our rules is that anything left out that should be put away results in making bedtime five minutes earlier the next night. So a pair of shoes can cost a child ten minutes. It works. Sometimes our kids complain that we're too strict, but more often than not, they let us know they appreciate it.

Discipline begins with parental self-discipline. You need to teach yourself to stop, look, and listen!

Your child has a minor mishap—spills juice or milk for the umpteenth time, perhaps. Stop. Try to remember what it was like to be his age. Does such a mistake deserve a reprimand or patience? Whatever action you choose, try to show God's love to your child through it.

Look. Figure out how to restore your child's confidence so that negative feelings aren't perpetuated.

Listen to what God is telling you so that you can comfort your child with understanding. Be mindful of how He has supported you when you have made mistakes.

What about spankings?

They keep you from screaming at your kids too much, are over quickly, and release you from the temptation of prolonged psychological abuse. Isn't that the reason we scream at our kids? Aren't we *really* saying—albeit at the top of our lungs—"Don't you realize that if you'll just do what I say the first or second or third time I say it, I won't have to belt you or paddle you or spank you, which is the last thing on earth I want to do?"

We never say those words, of course. And when the shouting

scene is over, we wonder, *Why did I do that? I don't scream at anyone else on the face of the earth—and never have—only at my children.*

◊ GLOW WORDS

It is easier to rule a kingdom than to regulate a family.

　　　　　　　　　　　　　　　　—Chinese proverb

But it's because we don't want to have to spank them. Right? Yes, it's right, but it's not valid reasoning. After all the other things we've talked about up to this point, it should be clear that yelling, shouting, screaming, whatever you want to call raising your voice so your child could hear you from the garage, is the worst possible form of discipline.

It's the worst possible form of anything. Attention? Yes, it's attention, but the totally negative kind, the type that only those children who get *no* other attention will accept.

If we think about it, spanking is much preferred over raising our voices at our kids. According to Dr. James Dobson, spanking should be reserved for willful disobedience, not for mistakes, not for childishness, not forgetfulness, and not because our children made us mad.

Spanking can provide loving as well as teaching opportunities. When a child knows he's going to get a spanking, he is scared. He is remorseful. He's tense. And he's all ears. He should know that you are calm and he should know precisely the nature of his willful disobedience as you see it. He should be told before and after that you love him and that you don't enjoy spanking him.

And a spanking should never physically injure a child. We feel it should be done only on the seat or the back of the legs. Some say you should use a neutral object so the child won't fear your hand, and others add that the hand is for loving. But God uses His hand to punish and to bless, and if you have a healthy relationship with your child, your hand will suffice without forever traumatizing him.

Of course it should hurt, and depending on the child, a stinging sensation can seem like an amputation. It should be unpleasant enough so that it is an eventuality to be avoided in the future, but it should be only severe enough to get the point across.

Often it's a good idea to get the child to communicate. "Do you know why you're going to get a spanking? Tell me why." Make sure he understands; otherwise, the discipline may be useless. Then afterward, "Why did I spank you? Do I like to spank you? Do you know I still love you, even when you disobey?"

Too many "authoritarian figures" want to provide punishment rather than discipline. As a perceptive executive once defined it: "Punishment is what happens when discipline fails."

Many people find that their children are the sweetest and most receptive after they have been spanked. We do. It's as if the child somehow innately knows that this ultimate form of focused attention came about because he was loved. He has been shown the proper boundaries; he knows who's in control, and he's comfortable with his place and acceptance in the family.

Even the youngest child will generally seek out the parent who administered the discipline and want to reestablish the relationship by sitting on the lap, snuggling, playing. And if the child doesn't, if he seems to withdraw and become sullen longer than would be normal after a spanking, seek him out. Reestablish the relationship yourself. Remind him, even if you did both before and after the spanking, "I still love you, you know."

Our kids often ask us to forgive them later. Sarah, however, will seek one of us out after a spanking and say, "I forgive you." It's always good for a laugh as we try to get her to turn the process around.

With the older children, we've found that you can't always

be fair in the truest sense of the word. Privileges differ. Ages differ. Punishment and discipline differ. It's our job to know what works with one and what works better with the other. And to know when we're getting our chains pulled.

We strongly believe you should never discipline a child in front of others—siblings included. Even in public you can take him or her aside.

Another tough lesson for us has been to discover that there's a big difference between being a loving, warm, personal parent and being a pal. We can't be pals to our kids. We're friends, but we're still in authority over them and they can't and shouldn't treat us like siblings or buddies from up the street. We sometimes catch our kids calling us names, as they would their friends. We nip that in the bud. There are ways to talk to kids and ways to talk to parents and other adults, and they need to know the difference. They're really happier with just a little respectful distance anyway.

◊ GLOW WORDS

The surest way to make life hard for your children is to make it soft for them.

—*Our Daily Bread*

Don't believe that discipline is a real need? Listen to this— even teenagers want to be disciplined, because they equate discipline with love. So assert Jane Norman and Myron Harris after conducting a three-year survey of over 160,000 American teenagers. The study was done in conjunction with Xerox Education Publications and Crossley Surveys.

"A fourteen-year-old girl said that she didn't think her mother loved her because she never got punished like her friends," according to Norman, who added, "She said she never got grounded."

Kids test us. They push at the fences of the corral. They want to know who's boss and what the limits are. They're secure in

knowing that we have definite guidelines, areas that must not
be crossed. Even Dr. Benjamin Spock, the beloved baby doctor
who advised two generations of parents to lighten up, has ad-
mitted that his advice on this score was faulty.

One way we can help ourselves and our children in this
matter of self-control is by seeking to control those aspects of
our environment that we perceive as destructive. We have a list
of things to limit or avoid that is short and sweet and probably
surprising. Would you have guessed television, toys, and bad
food?

Television

Vladimir Kosma Zworykin, one of the inventors of television, has been quoted, "I would never let my children get close
to this thing."

The evils of television are so well publicized by now that it's
almost too easy a target. The violence, the sex, the language,
the commercials, the zombielike response it elicits from every
member of the family are legend.

The American Academy of Pediatrics' Task Force on Children and Television states that repeated exposure to TV violence can make children not only accepting of real-life
violence, but also more violent themselves.

Yet television viewing is the single most time-consuming activity of children, after sleeping. Some would say kids' minds
are sleeping while they're watching, too.

Bill Bickley is a television producer. He should know what
he's talking about when he says: "When the country exhibits
such an overwhelming conservative response to a presidential
election, it tells me that the majority of Americans are coming
from a conservative perspective. Yet the majority of the people
involved in the entertainment industry, who are directly responsible for what's on television, are coming from the opposite perspective entirely. There are very few conservatives in
the entertainment industry."

We have a television, and we watch it. We are not addicted
to it. We don't "see what's on." We don't flip channels looking

for anything fun or interesting. At some point, it's crucial that a family, specifically parents, take charge of the TV set.

GLOW WORDS

The 23rd Channel

The TV set is my shepherd. My spiritual growth shall want.

It makes me to sit down and do nothing for His name's sake, because it requireth all of my spare time.

It keepeth me from doing my duty as a Christian, because it presenteth so many good shows that I must see.

It restoreth my knowledge of the things of the world and keepeth me from the study of God's Word.

It leadeth me in the paths of failing to attend the evening worship services and doing nothing in the kingdom of God.

Yea, though I live to be 100 I shall keep on viewing television as long as it will work, for it is my closest companion.

Its sounds and its picture, they comfort me.

It presenteth entertainment before me and keepeth me from doing important things with my family.

It fills my head with ideas which differ from those set forth in the Word of God.

Surely, no good thing will come of my life, because my television offereth me no good time to do the will of God; thus I will dwell crownless in the house of the Lord forever.

—Author Unknown

Is your family addicted to television? You can easily determine that by trying to go without it—just leave it off—for one full day. You might want to quit cold turkey for a few months. That's right. Just get rid of it, or store it. Give up the news, the soaps, the game shows, the sitcoms. You'll find things to do. Your family life will improve. Communication between family members will be healthier than ever.

Then, when you have it under control, when you know you can live without it, monitor it. Use your weekly television guide to mark those educational and socially redeeming programs you feel will benefit your family, and schedule them carefully.

We should worry as much or more about the behavior television prevents as we do about what behavior it produces. We'll talk more about its effect on creativity later.

Use a truly good television program as an incentive for children to finish chores and homework. Then you can make the event a real family activity with a snack, discussion, some snuggling, whatever.

"All television is educational television," says Nicholas Johnson, former United States Federal Communications Commissioner. "The only question is, What is it teaching?"

Some feel it is teaching kids that nothing is more important than what their friends think. There is tremendous peer pressure on children to watch and know every superhero, every cartoon, every kids' show. The choice is yours. Do you want them to be *in* and cool and knowledgeable, or do you want them to stand apart from the world and know how to think for themselves, to read, to create, to converse?

Author Kevin Perrotta, in *Taming the TV Habit* (Servant, 1982), says, "Violence and sex are not the only, or even the most serious, problems with television programming. The greater problems lie in the ways television nourishes non-Christian patterns of thinking about the world."

The boys and I like to watch ball games, and that can be

beneficial, but we're not glued to the set and we don't watch all day every day. It has been said that televised football is nothing more than sixty million people in easy chairs desperately needing exercise, watching twenty-two professional athletes desperately needing rest.

We're selective and we believe that any parent who feels the responsibility to control his own household can decide what will be watched and what will not.

How do you do it?

You just lay some ground rules. Some families say there is no television viewing without permission, and then there is no unsupervised watching. If that seems too severe, you might try letting the kids watch what you allow and trust them not to change the channels or to keep watching once that one show is over.

Would you rather your family not give in to the temptation to "see what's on"? What else is there to do?

Ideas from "Focus on the Family": "Play, build something, read, pray, walk, learn a craft, draw, paint, write, listen to music, make music, exercise, plan an outing, invite a friend over, listen to the radio, have a conversation, work a puzzle, bake something, do a good deed, go to bed."

Toys

We know this is the most surprising and controversial thing we'll say, but we have turned the evil eye on toys. We know, we know. It sounds cruel, barbaric, un-Christian. We're depriving our kids of everything everyone else has. Well, it works.

We get them books, educational products, clothes, functional things. Things they like and want and need. Things that will help them think and use their imaginations. It ties in with our new control over television. If they're not watching the mindless, violent superhero cartoons on television every Saturday morning and weekday afternoon, they aren't aware of all the trash that's offered by toy makers.

They hear about it at school, of course, but by now they're used to the fact that they don't get toys from us anymore. And they're none the worse for it.

Evaluate your last Christmas or a child's birthday. How long did he play with his favorite toy? How long did it last without breaking? If it stayed in good shape, does he still maintain interest in it?

Sure, there are certain special toys that some kids latch onto and use every day for months. But those are rare. Jill read a book called *Clutters Last Stand* by Don Aslett and it revolutionized our home. We de-clutter everyplace! We throw out unused things, mostly toys, but we don't limit it to toys.

Even the kids are into de-cluttering their rooms, dressers, and closets. Our home used to be cluttered with dozens and dozens and dozens of toys, broken and otherwise, mostly abandoned in one room or closet or another. Take the plunge. Try it. Get rid of such clutter. Kids are unbelievably creative.

No TV? No toys? My kids will rot! No, they won't. They'll grow up to be intelligent, active, earnest, interesting, conversant, well-read, people- and relationship-oriented. Sound impossible? Can you think of a more worthy cause?

Television, clutter, and toys can rob your kids of those virtues. The children could wind up with a gnawing need to be entertained, always reaching for the next buzz, the next high. Material things and TV foster a certain self-centeredness that is tough to cut through.

Our kids are happy and well-adjusted, and you know what? They don't even ask for toys anymore.

Bad Food

When Jimmy was about two years old, Jill realized that she might have an addiction to soda pop. By the middle of the morning, every morning, she just had to have a glass of pop. When she realized it, she decided to stop buying it, stop drinking it, stop needing it.

Only then did she realize that she had been hooked. Not drinking it was hard. Not buying it was strange. She wanted it more than ever, and that scared her. She was amazed that she could have become so dependent on something so seemingly minor.

Around the same time, I quit drinking my several soft drinks per basketball game. I lost a lot of weight almost overnight and felt much better. We both realized that the sugar and the caffeine had done a number on us.

We started reading about nutrition and the dangers of sugar and salt and preservatives and chemicals. Then a doctor friend, Paul Beals, mentioned casually that the average American adult doesn't really need red meats, beef and the like.

That struck a chord with us, and soon we were into healthy foods in a big way. We haven't cut out beef totally. Jill will still include ground beef in spaghetti, and the kids enjoy hamburgers occasionally.

But for the most part, we eat chicken and fish and fresh fruits and vegetables, whole grain breads, and sugarless treats. Of course, as the kids get older, it becomes harder and harder to monitor what they eat when they're away from home, but Jill can always tell when they've had some dessert at school. They come home wired.

There's more than enough evidence that healthy foods mean healthier children. For us, what food goes into their systems is as important as what goes into their brains. We can attest to the fact that our children have fewer headaches and stomachaches, fewer colds and fevers than average, and have excellent teeth and high energy.

A chilling story from our own experience drives this point home best. One of our boys has always been a little quiet. But he's also an unusually warm and sweet child and we rarely have any serious trouble with his behavior.

Yet late one spring he seemed to change overnight. He was sullen, crabby, rebellious. Simply not himself. When Jill started hearing from his teacher that his schoolwork was suffering and that he was disruptive in class, we knew something was seriously wrong.

He had never been a problem at school, but now his work was late or not turned in at all. Right during that time Jill heard a speaker talk about evidence of drug abuse in children. It scared her to death. He had all the symptoms. No energy. Listless. Lazy. Noncommunicative. Discourteous.

Jill couldn't think of any other possible causes. This was the kid who was an outstanding little athlete and who so enthusiastically threw himself into projects that he had sold more candy bars for the local baseball program than anyone else in the whole town. He won a beautiful ten-speed bicycle for his work.

Finally, Jill knew she had to search his room. It went against everything she believed and taught about privacy, but on the other hand, his well-being was the greater good and she was, after all, his mother.

She was staggered at what she found. No, there were no drugs, no needles, no weed. Just dozens and dozens and dozens of candy-bar wrappers. For every box he sold, he'd had a few bars for himself. The sugar, the caffeine, the fat had clogged his little system. In effect, he *was* on drugs.

When it became clear he had been found out, he was relieved. And within a few days of kicking the chocolate habit, he was back to his old self again.

Avoid junk food, too much beef, and all the additives. You'll be so happy and healthy and uncluttered and intelligent, you'll hardly recognize yourself!

GLOW WORDS

Correct your son, and he will give you comfort; he will also delight your soul.

—Proverbs 29:17

Yes, there are many sides to discipline—instruction, correction, punishment, control of the environment. Whatever our view on the subject, we should keep in mind the basic goals of discipline: self-control, maturity, the ability to make wise choices, respect for the authority of God. Lest you consider that controversy surrounding discipline in the home is something that has been raging only since Dr. Spock loosened the reins, consider this. On July 24, 1732, more than 250 years ago, Susannah Wesley wrote in a letter what she called her "Plan of education for my children."

In the excerpts to follow, you will notice a practice Mrs. Wesley termed "conquering their will" or "subjecting the will." Rebecca Lamar Harmon, author of *Susannah: Mother of the Wesleys* (Abingdon, 1968), explains that while "at first glance one might think this meant breaking the spirit of her children, nothing could be further from the truth. . . . Her system was always geared to a future when each individual child should have reached a state of maturity and could regulate his own life. The formation of character was ever the end of all her striving."

The author admits that Mrs. Wesley's methods seem "extremely hard and inflexible," but that compared to her contemporaries, she was actually mild. Her family was large (she bore nineteen children), and her regime was "not only for the more efficient handling of a large group, but also as better preparation for each family member for the battle of life ahead."

"Strength guided by kindness" ruled in the Wesley household, and the love Susannah had for each child is evidenced in the fact that she set aside a special time each week for each child.

Author Harmon points out: "Nowhere is there any record of resentment on the part of the Wesley children against their mother's method of education.

"In spite of the fact that Mrs. Wesley's system of education runs counter to the tenets of modern [secular] child guidance experts, it is worthy of study not only for historic interest but because her method worked. The children she reared developed into members of one of the most eminent families in English history, remarkable for their looks, their intellect, and their sterling character."

We agree. The Wesleys were great hymn writers, preachers, and authors. Following are excerpts from Susannah Wesley's letter:

The children were always put into a regular method of living, in such things as they were capable of, from their birth; as in dressing and undressing, changing their linen, etc.

When turned a year old (and some before) they were taught to fear the rod and to cry softly, by which means they escaped abundance of correction which they might otherwise have had, and that most odious noise of the crying of children was rarely heard in the house.

As soon as they were grown pretty strong, they were confined to three meals a day. They were never suffered to choose their meat, but always made to eat such things as were provided for the family. Drinking or eating between meals was never allowed, except in the case of sickness, which seldom happened.

In order to form the minds of children, the first thing to be done is conquer their will and bring them to an obedient temper. To inform the understanding is a work of time, and must with children proceed by slow degrees, as they are able to bear it; but the subjecting of the will is a thing which must be done at once, and the sooner the better, for by neglecting timely correction they will contract a stubbornness and obstinacy which are hardly ever after conquered, and never without using severity as would be as painful to me as to the child.

In the esteem of the world they pass for kind and indulgent whom I call cruel parents, who permit their children to get habits which they know must be afterwards broken. When a child is corrected, it must be conquered, and this will be no hard matter to do, if it be not grown headstrong by too much indulgence. And when the will of a child is totally subdued, and it is brought to revere and stand in awe of the parents, then a great many childish follies and inadvertencies may be passed by.

Some should be overlooked and taken no notice of, and others mildly reproved; but no willful transgression ought ever to be forgiven children without chastisement less or more, as the nature and circumstances of the case may require.

I insist on the conquering of the will of children betimes, because this is the only strong and rational foundation of a religious education, without which both precept and example will be ineffectual. But when this is thoroughly done, then a child is capable of being governed by the reason and piety of its parents, till its own understanding comes to maturity, and the principles of religion have taken root in the mind.

I cannot yet dismiss the subject. As self-will is the root of all sin and misery, so whatever cherishes this in children ensures their after wretchedness and irreligion; whatever checks and mortifies it, promotes their future happiness and piety. This is still more evident if we further consider that religion is nothing else than doing the will of God and not our own; that the one grand impediment to our temporal and eternal happiness being this self-will, no indulgence of it can be trivial, no denial unprofitable. Heaven or hell depends on this alone, so that the parent who studies to subdue it in his child works together with God in the renewing and saving a soul.

Our children were taught as soon as they could speak the Lord's prayer, which they were made to say at rising and bedtime constantly, to which, as they grew bigger, were added a short prayer for their parents, and some collects, a short catechism, and some portion of Scripture as their memories could bear.

They were quickly made to understand they might have nothing they cried for, and instructed to speak handsomely for what they wanted.

There were several by-laws observed among us. I mention them here because I think them useful.

1. It had been observed that cowardice and fear of punishment often lead children into lying till they get a custom of it which they cannot leave. To prevent this, a law was made that whoever was charged with a fault of which they were guilty, if

they would confess it and promise to amend, should not be beaten. This rule prevented a great deal of lying.

2. That no sinful action should ever pass unpunished.

3. That no child should be ever beat twice for the same fault, and that if he amended he should never be upbraided with it afterwards.

4. That every single act of obedience, especially when it crossed with their own inclinations, should be always commended, and frequently rewarded according to the merits of the case.

5. That if ever any child performed an act of obedience or did anything with an intention to please, though the performance was not well, yet the obedience and intention should be kindly accepted, and the child with sweetness directed how to do better for the future.

6. That propriety [the rights of property] be invariably preserved, and none suffered to invade the property of another in the smallest matter, though it were but of the value of a farthing or a pin, which they might not take from the owner without, much less against, his consent.

7. That promises be strictly observed; and a gift once bestowed, and so the right passed away from the donor, be not resumed. . . .

Poor Mrs. Wesley was born too soon! Wouldn't she be a hit in the Christian subculture today? She'd make the rounds of all the talk shows, write best-sellers, and become a media star!

Despite the quaintness of the Olde English, did you catch those of her ideas that remain popular today? Don't remind your child of his failure once he has been punished for it. Praise good actions, even good intentions. Ignore some childishness, but punish willful disobedience.

Sound familiar? These have become hot, new ideas during the last decade! The bottom line is common sense. Love equals discipline and discipline equals love. The parent who seems to love his child too much to correct him is doing him the greatest disservice of all. And the parent who might appear to some to be too strict, too picky, or too demanding is setting a standard for excellence and creating an atmosphere of loving security that will be the greatest gift the child can receive.

GLOW WORDS

There are two freedoms: the false where one is free to do what he likes, and the true where he is free to do what he ought.

—Charles Kingsley

A few days after two of our children had visited the pet shop with me, Jill discovered in one of their rooms a toy she didn't recognize. A quick investigation elicited a confession, along with the charge that the other child had also shoplifted a similar item from the pet shop.

We were horrified. Though the second accused didn't confess, the one who did was required to return the item to the store and make things right. The pet-shop owner was very good about it. He said he appreciated that the stolen item was returned, but he didn't treat it lightly. He told our child that it was serious and that it was against the law.

It was a good lesson, but we were doubly troubled a few weeks later when we discovered that, indeed, the other child had also taken something. Not only was he guilty of shoplifting, but also of lying about it when accused. I was embarrassed that I had to take yet another child back to make amends, but worse than that, we wondered what we were doing wrong if two of our children had shoplifted.

While we know that such behavior is a stage that many children go through, and also taking into consideration our fairly strict policies about toys and candy, we still chose not to treat the incident lightly and to take no shortcuts in the restitution process.

Sometimes the very results of a child's actions or irresponsibility are punishment enough. Such lessons can be very painful.

We love birds and have close to fifty of varying sizes and species. One of our boys was assigned the chore of feeding our new canaries, a couple of very expensive little beauties. When we questioned him about it, he kept saying, "Yes, yes, I will. Don't worry about it. I won't forget."

The birds were able to go without seed for a while, but they could last only a few hours without water. When we returned home from an outing late that night, Jill checked on the birds. All were fine except the two canaries. They were on their backs in the cage with their feet up. Dead.

The next morning, we had to break the news to the family, including the offender. We might have wished the lesson weren't so expensive and painful, but it certainly brought home the truth that when someone doesn't follow through on his commitments, there is a price. The price in this case included remorseful tears.

Through loving discipline responsible parents guide their children toward the self-control that is so essential to Christian maturity. But family life isn't all seriousness. It's what we do and you can do in your family environment to stimulate laughter, joy, creativity, and the making of memories that we discuss in the next chapter.

Chapter Seven

Unlocking Creativity in Your Children

> **God has planted the creative potential within our children. It is our duty—and what a joyous one—to let that creativity flourish in our homes.**
> —**Maxine Hancock,** *Creative, Confident Children*

In our family the keys to unlocking creativity in the children are enthusiasm, humor, spontaneity, and variety. Want your child's imagination to run wild? Want him to be unlimited in what his mind can conceive? It starts with you. That's where he takes his lead. Your encouragement and your response to your child's efforts are essential to the fulfillment of his creative potential.

Children are by nature imaginative. They love to "make believe." The younger the child, the crazier the stories that he likes. The older he grows, the more realistic he gets. Why is that? Why do older kids feel that fairy tales and silliness are for babies alone? Probably because we communicate it to them. If we want children who are truly imaginative, truly creative—and who doesn't?—we need first to break free from the grown-up shackles we've applied to our own minds. "Help children trust in their own thoughts and ideas," says Dr. Roger von Oech in *A Whack on the Side of the Head* (Warner Books, 1983). "Show them by your attitudes that getting ideas is a good thing."

Creativity, after all, is an imagining, questioning way of

thinking—a search for new ways of doing things. It involves an attitude or habit of mind that can be cultivated—or stifled.

Dr. von Oech continues, "Encourage and reward exploration. Invest some money each month in exploration. Visit a junkyard. Find history in a hardware store, fashion in an airport.

"Stockpile children with information.

"Take amazement in the world around you."

Not every creative endeavor has to be unusual. Some ideas just hark back to a slower era. Keep a junk box on hand, full of sewing scraps, pieces of paper, string, foil, buttons, whatever. When a child is bored, give him a sheet of construction paper, some glue, and the junk box and see what he can make of it.

Encourage your younger children to use their crayons to create their own pictures once in a while, rather than just coloring in the lines of coloring books. Be careful not to try to guess what their pictures are before they tell you. What you guess as a jet fighter might just be mom!

The host of "Mister Rogers' Neighborhood" (one TV show we endorse), Fred Rogers, says that we don't *have* to understand all of a child's creative efforts. What's important is that we communicate our respect for his attempts to express what's inside.

"Nothing legitimatizes young ideas like displaying them on the refrigerator door or framing them to hang at home or at the office. The four-year-old whose drawings are proudly displayed can feel as proud as the artist having a gallery showing."

See who can tell the tallest tale. You discourage lying, of course, but if your child is old enough to understand the difference between bearing false witness and just making up stories, he'll enjoy it. Start off by saying, "It was so cold last winter, we had to thaw our words before we could hear them!"

Then it's the child's turn. Keep trying to top each other with the wildest stories imaginable.

Does one of your children really enjoy words and word

games? Give him a word and see how many words he can come up with that rhyme with it. Let him challenge you with one.

Read one of your child's favorite books, then ask him to tell you what happened in the story before page one. Or after "The End."

Do your kids play dress up with mom and dad's clothes, or is that something that somehow went out of fashion when we grew up? Dig some things out of an old trunk and let them enjoy.

Make up a fairy tale together. Decide the characters in advance. A king and queen and a beautiful princess. A villain. You start and let your child make up every other line.

Draw crazy squiggles on a big piece of cardboard and let your child use it to make something recognizable, maybe a car or an animal.

Fred Rogers says that the toddler's first role model is "usually mother as she goes about her housekeeping. Since very young children's creativity is often expressed in 'smearing,' giving a child a rag dipped in water and letting him 'wash' the floor with her, or giving him a small lump of cookie dough as she bakes so he can pat it, roll it, and smear it is the beginning of enjoying creativity."

Pat likes to say that if you don't think creativity is still alive in children, watch a five-year-old make a peanut butter and jelly sandwich.

Supporting your children's creative activities and responding to them with constructive praise are two of the most important things you can do for them. Respect for a child's individuality is essential. Encourage all types of activities. It may be hard for artistic parents to express enthusiasm for the efforts of a child who is mechanically inclined. Or for the athletic parent to get excited about poetry-writing offspring. But to stifle a child's natural bent and insist he follow his parents' interests may turn that child off completely. Let the child move at his own pace. There's a delicate balance to be maintained between encouraging a child to reach out and tackle a challenging task and pushing him too hard—and once again risking turning him off.

Don't set unreasonable standards or be overly critical—even in jest. Derogatory remarks often stay with a child much longer than we realize.

Even teachers, unfortunately, can be killers of creativity. Children, especially at the elementary level, so look up to their teachers that the smallest unthinking remark or gesture can hurt the child.

Harry Chapin wrote a song in 1978 that beautifully and sadly illustrates this truth. It's called *Flowers Are Red*:

> The little boy went first day of school
> He got some crayons and started to draw
> He put colors all over the paper
> For colors was what he saw
> And the teacher said . . . What you doin' young man?
> I'm paintin' flowers he said
> She said . . . It's not the time for art young man
> And anyway flowers are green and red
> There's a time for everything young man
> And a way it should be done
> You've got to show concern for everyone else
> For you're not the only one
> And she said . . .
>
> Flowers are red young man
> Green leaves are green
> There's no need to see flowers any other way
> Than the way they have always been seen
>
> But the little boy said . . .
> There are so many colors in the rainbow
> So many colors in the mornin' sun
> So many colors in a flower and I see every one
> Well teacher said . . . you're sassy
> There's ways that things should be
> And you'll paint flowers the way they were
> So repeat after me . . .
> And she said . . .
> There's no need to see flowers any other way
> Than the way they always have been seen

But the little boy said . . .
There are so many colors in the rainbow
So many colors in the morning sun
So many colors in a flower
And I see every one
The teacher put him in a corner
She said . . . It's for your own good
And you won't come out 'til you get it right
And all responding like you should
Well finally he got lonely
Frightened thoughts filled his head
And he went up to the teacher
And this is what he said . . . and he said

Flowers are red, green leaves are green
There's no need to see flowers any other way
Than the way they always have been seen

Time went by like it always does
And they moved to another town
And the little boy went to another school
And this is what he found
The teacher there was smilin'
She said . . . Painting should be fun
And there are so many colors in a flower
So let's use every one
But that little boy painted flowers
In neat rows of green and red
And when the teacher asked him why
This is what he said . . . and he said . . .

Flowers are red, green leaves are green
There's no need to see flowers any other way
Than the way they always have been seen

One of the greatest Christian musicians ever, a man who has thrilled audiences for decades with his vocal and instrumental genius, has never gotten over a comment made by his third grade teacher. She told him, "You are the dumbest student I've ever had."

We realize that such an unthinking remark by a teacher is rare and that any modern, self-respecting educator would know better. Yet a friend of ours still remembers an incident nearly twenty-five years ago when his sixth-grade teacher showed his handwritten paper to the whole class on an opaque projector and ridiculed the way he added flair to his signature.

Few people back then, the student included, thought about the significance of such things. That they were evidences of creativity and uniqueness; that a child might be trying to stand out from several kids in a big family, or even a big class. No, it was just something out of the ordinary and had to be discouraged.

Don't be guilty of the same thing. If your child wants to sign his name like John Hancock, let him experiment. Don't squelch it. Model creativity.

Let's stop for a minute and consider a few more hindrances to creativity. One is television watching, which we just discussed in the last chapter. For now, simply consider the way your child appears when he's sitting before the tube.

Is he thinking? Is he doing? Is he imagining? Is anything at all left for him to do but drink it in? One of the first things to do in unlocking your child's creativity is to replace with other activities much of the TV he watches.

Letting the children watch television from the time they get home from school until dinner is one way to put their minds in neutral. Then it's a little homework after dinner and back to the TV where mom and dad join them until bedtime. And then how does it go? Getting the kids to bed is a rush job during commercials. Creative.

If you want to wean your child slowly from media, let him listen to dramatic tapes of children's stories. You can find recordings of the classics, which will be educational while naturally forcing him to imagine scenes in his mind rather than having them staged and produced and delivered to his eyes.

Another hindrance to creativity is overscheduling. We all want our kids to be active and productive and fulfilled, but is it necessary to have something structured for them every moment? They can become so busy they don't have a free minute to think for themselves.

We know a man who has a house rule. Every person in the family is required—*required,* mind you, not just *allowed*—to spend an hour a day by himself. That's mom, dad, and each child. He says the family members appreciate each other more, fight less, talk more, and seem calmer and more self-contained than before.

One child used the time for a nap after school until he found it was interfering with his sleep at night. So he began reading. His sister listened to the radio for the first week until it bored her and gave her the uneasy feeling she was wasting time. So, she did her homework during the first hour she was home from school and was able to enjoy the rest of the evening, no matter what came up.

Another way of stifling creativity in kids is by making life too easy for them, by choosing their clothes, never letting them make their own lunches, by doing the difficult chores for them. Building your children's confidence is an important element in unlocking their creativity. They can't build confidence if they're not given responsibility.

GLOW WORDS

Laughter is the hand of God on the shoulder
of a troubled world.
—Charlie "Tremendous" Jones

Even with chores and responsibility childhood is hardly unendurable! Imagine what the addition of heavy doses of humor will give your child. If humor can make tough things easier, it can make a happy home happier. Nichele Miller discusses this in "Laughing Your Way to Health and Healthy Relationships." (*Family Life Today,* February, 1984).

Last year we had the opportunity to make videotapes of our vacation at Blue Lake, Wisconsin. During a particularly tranquil morning, my husband was fortunate enough to capture (with full sound effects) my sudden unplanned departure from an inner tube, in the form of a back flip.

We recently had the pleasure of reviewing this spectacle. Everyone roared, and I managed a few weak grins myself, even though on tape I resembled an unhappy whale trying to beach itself.

A friend, who is self-admittedly much too old and out of shape for such shenanigans, will wallow in the deep snow with his elementary school-age boys at the drop of a hat. The first time it happened the kids were so shocked that they just watched. Then they started playing snow football, tackling each other and rolling around as if they were all under ten. Dad wasn't!

"Man, that was fun!" the eight-year-old told his mother when he finally went into the house to get warm. They still talk about it.

The bottom line is this: Your life will be more balanced and fulfilled if you give time to playing with your kids—ten minutes of wrestling before dinner; family night of Monopoly; a bedtime story; and especially "work-play" projects like cleaning up the backyard or washing the car. You'll live longer for it.

Remember the craziest thing that ever happened in your house? Did your father, wrestling with your brothers, fall into the bathtub? Did your mother play a practical joke? Tell these stories to your kids? Better yet, reenact them.

Does your child ever pretend to shoot you in his game of cowboys and Indians? If you see him coming, plan to fall right out of your chair onto the floor, letting the newspaper or the mail or whatever is in your hand go flying. Your spouse can tell him that only a kiss will wake you up.

Author Norman Cousins has proved that the old adage "Laughter is good medicine" (which is stated in other phrasing in Proverbs 17:22 as well) is true. His book *Anatomy of an Ill-*

ness tells of his belief that laughter therapy cured him of a debilitating illness.

With my good friend Ken Hussar I wrote *Nothing But Winners* (Trimark, 1984), a collection of six thousand humorous one-liners. Imagine Jill's and my surprise when twelve-year-old Jim began memorizing them and sprinkling them into his daily conversations.

Note that we're talking here about creativity, the imagination, the pockets of possibilities in the human mind. We're not saying that the end-all goal for parents is to provide children with pleasure and happiness. For one thing, you can't do that. The only person who can give your child abundant life is Jesus Christ, and the New Testament is clear that that is not necessarily a life of only fun and pleasure either.

None of us wants our children to be *un*happy, of course. But happiness comes from the pursuit of something else. The person who pursues happiness for its own sake will be disappointed. True joy and contentment and pleasure come from doing things for other people, for God, for family, for church, for community. We need to be careful that we don't inadvertently teach our children to overvalue happiness in itself.

What we're talking about here is growing creative kids. Not producing fun junkies.

Where did parents, especially Christian parents, get the idea that life should offer their children a perpetual round of entertainment? What values do these parents think they are teaching?

"True happiness," writes Rebecca Lyon in *Psychology for Living,* "can be obtained only as a by-product of responsible, productive, Christ-centered living. If one takes such an admittedly radical philosophy seriously (as true Christians must), then it necessarily follows that some parents are unwittingly steering their children in the wrong direction."

Just doing things together, funny or not, creates memories for kids and opens their minds. Just as your car needs a periodic tune-up and your house needs freshening-up maintenance, so your family needs a recreational fix to renew and keep it operative. We've talked about the importance to family relationships of spending time together as a family. But family activities can also provide a tremendous stimulus to creativity as well. And don't forget that the more varied a child's experiences, the better adjusted he usually is.

There's always a spiritual emphasis in our home, but we try to keep the rest of our activities diversified. Here are some of the ways we work in recreational tune-ups.

1. *Family Night.* Let family members take turns choosing what the whole family will do together. It can be sports, music, crafts, games. It can be hospitality—entertaining or visiting. It can serve others—visiting the sick, welcoming newcomers. There's no end to the possibilities. If a once-a-week Family Night is unrealistic for you, try for every other week or once a month.

2. *Family Day.* This is an enlarged version of Family Night that extends the range of activities. Spend the day exploring a nearby city or the countryside. Visit a museum, go on a nature walk, take up a new sport. Occasionally taking along a disadvantaged child who might not otherwise have the opportunity can enrich your children's lives as well as the guest's.

Although Family Day will usually be on the weekend, what a great opportunity for dad to surprise everyone by taking an impromptu day off to spend with the family.

3. *Minivacations.* Too often we think only of the all-or-nothing week or two-week vacation. The change of pace of a weekend holiday can really be restorative—especially during the winter months when we spend longer periods of time indoors. Many of the newspapers feature columns on "short hops," points of interest within a one- or two-hundred-mile area.

Too often parents rely on the school system to provide the children's "field trips," forgetting that such outings can be fun and instructional for the whole family.

How well do you really know your child? When your first-grader came home with one of those handmade "autobiog-

unforgettable time that the kids still occa-
. We encouraged them to express their own
uld guard against hidden concerns. Jim told
the birth might have hurt her. She thought,
utie!, but she also was able to impress upon
in is a small price for the miracle of the new

lot about the blood, reminding herself that it
, not bad blood. Life-giving blood, not a
for the baby, so it was all right, wasn't it,

Jill, "Was I in your tummy before I was born,

re in another lady's tummy in Korea, just like
the whole issue of adoption came up in a natu-
vay.

is everybody's baby. And our family has a "to-
y" that will bond us forever. Even Michael will
about that family experience, our first with all
present."

his gave our children a view of the miraculous, an
n by God. If seeing a child born before their eyes
ribute to unlocking their own sense of awe and cre-
on't know what will.

ime passes quickly. A day happens just once in
e. A moment, an experience, comes and goes. But a
childhood memory—can mold a future.

raphies" listing his favorite food, favorite color, best friend—
illustrated with crayoned artwork—you probably knew all the
"answers." But what about some other questions that might be
asked? What is his biggest fear? or embarrassment? Do you
know the answers to those questions? And as your child has
grown older have you kept pace? Do you still know what
makes him tick?

In order to really understand your child, to help and support
him, to bring out his creativity, you need to know him. We've
seen lists of questions used in counseling, lists of questions in
memory books, lists of questions for use in Family Fun Nights.
(How would you score as far as your child's likes and needs are
concerned? And, turning the tables, how well do they know
you?) Whether you consider it a serious learning experience or
just a gimmick for fun, see how you do on these questions—
and add some of your own.

1. What is your child's favorite food?
2. What is his favorite pastime?
3. What is he afraid of?
4. What is his favorite TV program?
5. What is his favorite book?
6. Who is his best friend?
7. Who does your child admire?
8. What does he like best, and least, about school?
9. What is your child's favorite toy?
10. What is his most-prized possession?
11. What does your child like best about you?
12. What do you do that upsets your child?
13. What does your child want to do when he grows up?
14. What would your child consider a special treat?
15. Does your child get along well with other children?
16. If not, do you know why?
17. Is there anything your child especially dislikes or dreads
    doing?
18. Has your child had any major disappointments?
19. What is your child's favorite holiday or family occasion?
20. Of what is your child most proud?

One of the best ways we know of unleashing the creative imaginations of children is by doing things as a family that they will always remember. Memories give us all a sense of belonging. No doubt many of your fondest childhood memories revolve around family vacations and holidays. Such activities help create a sense of permanence and bring families closer, but don't limit heritage-building experiences to holidays. We've listed some suggestions here, but don't limit yourself to them. Make your own memory-builders.

1. Keep a journal of your family's special events and accomplishments and review them once a year—on New Year's Day for example.
2. Establish traditions that are carried on year after year. A Fourth of July picnic or decorating the Christmas tree, for example, can become very special family occasions. Involve each family member in a way that causes him to look forward to the event each year.
3. Make a family tree, going back as far as possible. Keep it current with new information.
4. Start a photo album for each child, with pictures of themselves and of relatives. Then, with a little help from you, encourage them to keep it going. Better yet, have the child add a sentence or two of commentary for the photos.
5. Record your children's early years in letters you write to them. When they're old enough, make them a present of the letters.
6. Give each child a keepsake box. Make sure he understands this is a place for keeping special treasures, not a place for stashing toys. You might start this off with a family memento.

Keeping track, making books of remembrance, telling family stories that happened before a child was old enough to remember, all can be memory builders. Tell him, instead of a made-up bedtime story, the true account of how you and your spouse met, what you thought of each other at first, how you

fell in love.
that God ha
you. Childrei
When Jill w
we wanted to i
rience they wo
long to all of us
The hospital I
the delivery room
exception for Sar
whole 76ers team
We realize that i
tire family in the cl
of personal preferei
with our children th
felt confident that the
Believing strongly t.
the parents, we had al
mation as was approp
Preparing for Michael's
to have many discussion
uncontrived way. And as
dren that these gifts from
responsibility.
We all attended classes
informed about everything
happening. The kids were to
day, they would be involved.
When the big day arrived,
come after noon. Jim and Bo
Sarah and I trooped into the de
strategically so we could all see
The little ones were coloring
and then, of course, they were all
hard, and right in the middle of tl
"Daddy, move!"
I was in Sarah's way. She didn't

130

It was a special,
sionally talk about
reactions so we co
Jill he was afraid
Good thinking, C
him how such pa
baby.
Karyn talked
was good blood
wound. "It was
Mommy?"
Sarah asked
like Michael?"
"No, you we
Andrea." And
ral, beautiful
So, Michae
gether memor
enjoy hearing
six children
We hope t
act of creatic
doesn't conti
ativity, we c

Summer
your lifetin
memory—

Chapter Eight

Modeling

> Every parent must develop a sowing mentality, a realization that literally everything he does or says is a seed of some kind, sown in some soil.
> —Pat Hershey Owen, *The Genesis Principle for Parents*

Wouldn't it be fun to know what your children will be like when they grow up? Will he look like dad? Will she look like mom? What will their values be? How will they act? How will they raise *their* children?

You can get a pretty good idea by looking in the mirror. What are your values? How do you act? How do you raise your children? Do you find yourself saying things to your kids that you vowed you'd never say? Like:

"Because I said so, that's why!"

"I don't always have to have a reason."

"When I was a kid, we respected our parents!"

"No more of your backtalk!"

"How many times do I have to tell you?"

GLOW WORDS

Relationships always precede rules. In fact, they are more important than rules. The principle: a child tends to accept your ideas, your philosophy, because he accepts you.

—Howard Hendricks, *Heaven Help the Home!*

One thing we need to face is that we are models to our children, whether we mean to be or not. Good or bad, what they see is what we're gonna get. There are some kids who grow up and improve on areas in which their parents were weak. Perhaps dad worked too much and was home too little. His son could make a concerted effort to change that.

Children are natural mimics—they act like their parents in spite of every attempt to teach them good manners!

Perhaps mom was not as physically or verbally affectionate as she could have been. Her daughter could be a better mother in that way. But for the most part, we're turning out little carbon copies of ourselves.

Fred Smith in *You and Your Network* says, "Our function as parents is to build into our children a sense of responsibility which will eventually release them from our guidance."

Dr. Reuben Archer Torrey, evangelist, pastor, Bible teacher, and author, said, "A man's success as a Christian leader will not be determined until one sees his grandchildren."

That can be scary or exhilarating, depending upon how we view ourselves. It's not too late to be the models we would have wanted to have, had we been able to choose.

Pat Hershey Owen, in her book *The Genesis Principle for Parents* (Tyndale, 1985), writes:

"Every parent must develop a sowing mentality, a realization that literally everything he does or says is a seed of some kind, sown in some soil. As a parent, as a human being, I must continually be aware of the kinds of seeds I am sowing. Not until I am conscious of my actions will I be able to plant seeds that will positively benefit myself, my family, and God's kingdom. We cannot choose whether or not to plant. We can only choose our seeds."

She goes on to describe spiritual nutrients to equip parent and child for future growth in the Lord and to "help prevent possible cross-pollinating by the sowing of negative seeds." They are simple: prayer and the Bible.

Do your kids see and hear you pray other than at mealtimes or in church? Is your Bible cover faded and are the pages dog-eared from so much use? If so, you should be able to count on your son or daughter wearing out a few Bibles on their way to maturity. If not, they may wind up just weekend Christians like mom and dad.

The ten behaviors kids want most from their parents were identified in an interview with 100,000 children, ages eight to fourteen, from twenty-four countries and varied social backgrounds. According to an article in the *First Baptist Reminder,* children reported that they:

1. Didn't want parents to argue in front of them.
2. Wanted to be treated with the same affection as other children in the family.
3. Didn't want to be lied to.
4. Wanted mutual tolerance from both parents.
5. Wanted friends welcome in the home.
6. Wanted comradeship with parents.
7. Wanted parents to answer questions.
8. Didn't want to be punished in front of neighborhood kids.
9. Wanted parents to concentrate on their good points, not weaknesses.
10. Wanted parents to be constant in their affections and moods.

Have you ever made a conscious effort to think about just what behaviors you want to develop in your children? These are some of the things we would like to instill in ours:

Obedience to God
Honesty
Loyalty
Keeping of one's word
Responsibility for chores and goals
Unselfish giving to others
Kindness and consideration of others
Respect for the property of others
Development and discriminating use of talents (and time)

Take a look at your own list. Then take a look at yourself.

Are you modeling the characteristics you want to see in your children?

We were really pleased the day that Bobby talked to Jill about the kids he wanted to invite to his birthday party. "Is it all right if I invite _____? He doesn't have a father, and no one ever invites him to parties."

Of course we encouraged him to invite the child. The boy was a "problem child," but we understood some of the reasons, and we were happy that something positive had gotten through and that Bobby had exhibited such compassion.

Charles Swindoll says he wants to leave his kids with a strong sense of self-worth and confidence. "If I'm gone out of their lives tomorrow, I want their lasting memory to be, 'Here was a man who believed in me and was committed to my future, even if it were very different from his.'

"My greatest announcement to the world is really my kids. I think that makes or breaks what I talk about."

We like to provide for our kids a model of hospitality. We want them to see us entertaining Christian workers whenever possible. That way, the children get the benefit of helping serve God's ministers and also, we hope, learning Christian principles from them.

Occasionally we will take the responsibility of finding housing in our area for 150 kids from Word of Life, and we always take several of them into our own home. When schedules and plans break down, we often wind up with more than it seems we can take, but our kids know our motto: There's always room for one more.

One year, with kids sleeping in the hallways and on the floor, the house was full of our own family and Word of Life people. I was on a kick of asking everyone what their favorite verse was so I could memorize it. As part of my memorizing a verse a day I like to link them with a person or even a sermon.

One of the girls, Loretta MacDonald, from South Carolina, told me her verse, Colossians 3:2, "Set your affection on things above, not on things on the earth," which I later memorized.

Months later, when we were at Word of Life Camp in Schroon Lake, New York, we ran into Loretta. I remembered her name and her verse.

Loretta was greatly impressed, and friendship developed between us. Eventually, she became our ministry secretary in New Jersey.

A friend of ours served on the staff at a Christian camp one summer. After a ball game one evening he and a few colleagues were waiting in the parking lot for the special speaker for the next day to arrive.

As they waited, the sun sank and the mosquitoes attacked. They left the glow of the street lamp illuminating the parking lot to head into the fellowship hall, but the sound of a fast car approaching made them turn. They were in the shadows between the light and the building, unable to be seen.

The car slid to a stop and the driver leaped out, spitting a list of euphemisms for swear words that left little doubt about what he meant. "For cripes sake, Timmy! What'sa matter with you! Gosh darn it! Look at my pants!"

The driver was brushing ice and pop off his trousers as his wife scurried around with some tissues. He waved her off. "Just forget it! Geez! I told you to be careful with that root beer!"

"I'm sorry, Dad! It was an accident!"

"Oh, sure! Is that what I'm supposed to tell someone when it looks like I've wet my pants here?"

The wife let out a chuckle she quickly regretted. "Oh, you're just great!" he shouted. "You don't have root beer all over you!"

"All right, John, now let's calm down and find our cabin."

"You find it! Tell 'em anything you want, but I'm waitin' in the car until we're ready to move in."

"Can I go with Mom, Dad?"

"I wish you would!"

The next morning the same man gave an impressive Bible study to the whole camp population. He was mild, he was cool, he was calm, he was articulate. He and his wife and young son stood by the door of the chapel as campers and staff filed out. He smiled and shook hands, and when the compliments came he looked up and pointed up and said, "Praise the Lord."

Of course, some of those staffers slipped past without greeting him or shaking his hand. They looked carefully at the wife and son who were smiling and obviously proud of their husband and father, but whose eyes and lips showed the secret strain of living with a man with such a short fuse.

During the evening meeting, while the man held forth impressively again, the wife and son planned to drive into town for a few things. One of the camp staffers was in the parking lot again as they climbed into the car. Just as the woman was carefully backing out, a car pulling in turned too sharp and scraped the side of her car. It was a minor scratch, but of course, both drivers were upset.

As the woman in the offending car sat with her head in her hands, the little boy jumped from the passenger's side of his parents' car and began berating her. "Gosh darn it! I can't believe it!" He stomped around with his hands on his hips. He bent over at the waist and stared at the scratch in the paint, then turned and kicked the other driver's door.

His mother got out and grabbed him by the neck with one hand. "That's enough!" she said. "I take this from your father, but I won't take it from you!"

She yanked him back around to the other side of the car and shoved him in, then dealt kindly with the other woman. The camp staffer went with her and her son back to the chapel where she later told her husband that they had still not gone to town because there had been a little accident in the parking lot.

"I'm sure it was nothing major," he said, smiling benignly. "You're both okay?"

She nodded, looking relieved that she had been able to tell him in front of someone. The boy moved close to his father. "It was the other woman's fault, Dad. I told her off."

"Oh, that wasn't necessary," the man said. "I'm sure it was just an accident."

Later that evening, after dark, the man went out by himself and squatted next to the rear fender of his car. In the light from the street lamp he could make out the long scratch. He stepped back and kicked his car so hard that he injured his foot and hobbled toward his cabin. For the rest of the week, he limped around, explaining simply that he had a sore foot.

The sad fact is that the mother was wrong. She said she would not take it from her son. But she would. For the rest of his life. Because it was programmed into him.

The boy's father had gifts and abilities and probably even a heart for the Lord. But his weak spot, his temper, was only the start of the bad modeling job he was doing. It was compounded by his hypocrisy. He had a public and private persona—of course, we all do, but they are not typically so widely diverse—and it sent confusing signals to his son.

One can imagine that when the son grew up, the signals were not so confusing. They were crystal clear. You acted one way in front of people and another in front of your own family. The son eventually tired of the sham in his own life and left the church, beginning a string of personal disappointments that plague him to this day.

Our friend reports that most of the staffers who witnessed these incidents were from solid homes and churches and simply learned a valuable lesson from what they saw. But there was a new Christian among them. One with many questions and doubts. They lost him that week. He, surely unfairly, painted all Christians with the same brush and said he couldn't handle the two-facedness.

Like the son, he was a victim. A casualty.

Modeling is a terribly difficult responsibility, because we are doing it all the time, whether we intend to or not. And our children are watching and being programmed, whether they know it or not. A four-year-old doesn't consciously record the fact that she never hears mom pray or sees her with her Bible except in church. That seed merely gets planted.

There is a story about ancient China that Jill likes, where the people desired security from the barbaric hordes to the north; so they built the Great Wall. It was so high they knew no one could climb over it and so thick that nothing could break it down.

They settled back to enjoy their security.

During the first years of the wall's existence, China was invaded three times. Not once did the barbaric hordes break down the wall or climb over the top. Each time they bribed a gatekeeper and then marched right through the gates.

The Chinese were so busy relying upon the walls of stone that they forgot to teach integrity to their children.

Compare that story with the one John Maxwell tells from his childhood:

"One day the junior boys' Sunday school teacher stopped in the middle of his lesson and said, 'Boys, I pray for you every day. Right after class, I need to see Steve Banner, Phil Conrad, Junior Fowler, and John Maxwell.'

"After class the four of us huddled in the corner with our teacher. 'Last night while I was praying for you, I sensed that the Lord was going to call each of you into full-time Christian service. I want to be the first to encourage you to obey God.'

"Then he wept as he prayed, asking the Lord to use us for His glory. Today we all pastor churches. Sunday school teachers made a positive mark on my life because of their acceptance and affirmation."

Pray that God will make you vigilant. Look for ways to be Christ-like around your children. Guard those idle moments when you feel no message is being sent, because some message is *always* being sent.

There is also such a thing as reverse modeling. Tim Hansel, in *Enough Is More Than Enough,* says he has learned volumes merely from watching children play. "Some of the things my midget gurus have taught me:

"*Total immersion.* They do it with their whole selves.

"*Total concentration.*

"*New perspectives.* They are real, down to earth, fresh, innocent, and un-*adult*-erated.

"*Ability to bounce back*. They are flexible, resilient.

"*Total honesty of expression*. When they are happy, they laugh. When they are frustrated, their anger is undiluted. When they cry, they are sadness incarnate.

"Every day I realize more and more that we have something to learn from these tiny encyclopedias of life."

Someone has said that to really know a man, observe his behavior with a woman, a flat tire, and a child. Tommy Lasorda, the colorful manager of the Los Angeles Dodgers, was a model to me in this several years ago. Jimmy, four at the time, was with me when I spoke at the Dodgers' chapel service when they were in town to play the Phillies. They were all sitting around eating doughnuts.

Right during my message, Jimmy, feeling very much at home and close to me, piped up, "Daddy! I want a doughnut!"

I kept on talking, knowing that time was limited and the attention spans of nervous ballplayers short. Meanwhile, Tommy Lasorda left the room and hurried back with a huge, jelly-filled doughnut for Jimmy.

Last spring, Jill discovered a book review Jimmy had done for his sixth-grade class at Bethel Baptist Christian School. The assignment had been to review any autobiography. Without our knowing it, he chose *The Gingerbread Man,* and wrote all about the main character without naming him until the end.

It began, "The man was tall and slightly overweight with long, black sideburns. . . ." Jimmy highlighted the story, telling that the man's job was to get people to come to basketball games. He outlined some of the ways the main character did this.

Jimmy wrote that when the man became a Christian, he switched from trying to be rich and successful to caring more about trying to be like God. He finished, "He has had a great influence on my life, and when I grow up, I want to be just like my dad, Pat Williams."

The next two chapters take a closer look at Fathering and Mothering. We hope both parents will read both chapters.

You'll notice that the fathering chapter is longer. It seems more commitment is needed from fathers today and they have more to learn. Also, the family-minded father is in vogue, so, more material has been produced about fathering! Supposedly, women already know how to be good mothers. It's the men who need the most help. See what you think.

Chapter Nine

Fathering

As fathers, we need to learn how to provide a balance of
love and discipline. We need to be firm, but also compas-
sionate. I believe that our children should regard us as a
shelter, that we are the first place any of our family members turn for help when they are facing a predicament.
They need to know that we are the "orderkeeper."
                                                —Paul Lewis
                                        How Can a Father Win?

"The husband who will take full, total, overall responsibility
for his family, and take the initiative in conveying his love to
his wife and children, will experience unbelievable rewards: a
loving, appreciative, helping wife who will be her loveliest for
him; children who are safe, secure, content and able to grow to
be their best. . . . Fathers," writes Dr. Ross Campbell in *How to
Really Love Your Child,* "the initiative must be ours."
Since our marriage was rekindled and I have consciously
worked at Blessing, Edifying, Sharing, and Touching, this initiative has extended to the growing family as well. Now, rather
than rushing outside for a hurried, impatient, frustrating catch
with the boys, I try to give them whatever time they require for
playing, talking, jogging, or just doing nothing. The kids, I hope,
no longer feel they are intruding upon my daily schedule.
Louis Evans, in *Bold Commitment,* writes, "When Christ
created each member of a family with creative potential, He
didn't expect that potential to be buried under a blanket of re-
strictions or hidden in a closet of frustrations. He did not mean

for a wife, or children, to submit to a false authority rooted in an unhealthy or insecure male ego. No entity is better suited than the family to bring about human development, and that is the responsibility of the head of the home.

"Who's in charge here? *Jesus Christ.* And in reverence to Him, a husband—a servant-head to his wife and children, sacrificing for their development—and a wife, exercising the authority that accompanies her gifts, ministering to her husband, her children, and her world. As these two grow together, under Christ, they become the exciting, mature persons the world is 'standing on tiptoe . . . to see coming into their own' (Romans 8:19, PH)."

I like to collect advice on how to be a better parent. Once I asked Bob Ferry, general manager of the Washington Bullets, whose two grown sons and daughter are good kids and unusually close to each other and to their parents, "If you could list the things that made you a successful father, what would they be?"

"Three things, Pat. First, I married the right woman. Second, I married the right woman. Third, I married the right woman."

That was a nice compliment to his wife, Rita, but then he elaborated about two other things that really stuck with me. "One, we found our children's strengths—the things they did best—and we focused in on them. We did everything we could to allow them to achieve maximum success in those areas. (Both sons have been outstanding collegiate basketball players at Harvard and Duke.)

"Two, by doing this, something positive happened that we had not planned. In driving them to their various activities over the years, it seemed we were constantly in the car with them. That gave us lots of one-on-one time with them."

Apparently that led to open communication, fewer adolescent problems, and better relationships, now that the kids are older.

"I have never particularly enjoyed being an authority for anyone, especially for my children," says Dr. Ross Campbell in *How to Really Love Your Teenager* (Victor Books, 1982). "I too am tempted to treat my children as contemporary friends, but I dare not. Yes, I am loving and friendly with them and enjoy laughing and having fun. And on occasion, I will share appropriate personal information with them, but only for their educational benefit—*not for my emotional benefit.*

"I must not forget that I am their father and that they need my authority and direction. If I relinquish or neglect my responsibility for being the authority in the home—along with Pat [his wife], for she too must assume her position of authority—my children will not be happy. They will feel insecure, and will be very apt to develop poor behavior patterns.

"As parents, our first responsibility is to make our children feel genuinely loved. Our second responsibility is to be authority figures for our children and to lovingly discipline them."

Most fathers are proud of their children and of their children's accomplishments. They go out of their way to support their little athletes, ballet dancers, poets, and so forth, and in that way attempt to show their love. But it's not enough. More is required. Fathers must *express* affection.

Dr. Paul Meier of the Minirth-Meier Clinic says that most homosexuals crave their father's affection that they never received as a child. "They really want to be loved by their fathers and end up seeking the affection of other men. Ages three through six are particularly critical in forming a child's sexual identity."

In our family, we have found that a love initiative toward the children is required on a practical basis as well. In other words, I can't just support the kids in their various athletic and artistic endeavors. My joke to Jill is, "I got you into this mess (i.e., a house full of kids), so I should help you out." I do this by trying to really be home when I'm home. I go through the entire bedtime routine with each child whenever possible, getting them from the bathroom to the bed and spending time chatting and praying with them and getting them settled.

My own father, James Williams, was a typical proud poppa.

He came to my baseball games and was so enthusiastic that I often felt embarrassed. Once I even directed him to the wrong baseball diamond to avoid having him at the game. Another time Dad brought popsicles for everyone on the team, and I was stuck with the nickname "Popsicle" for a few weeks, suffering from that typical teenage embarrassment over one's parents.

Years later on my last day at Wake Forest, in 1962, our team was eliminated from the NCAA baseball tournament. Dad was there and worried about how I was taking it. But I wasn't in the mood to talk, and after a few brief, noncommittal words with him, I started the long trip home with my buddies from North Carolina to Delaware.

I never saw my father alive again. He was killed in an accident on the way home. He didn't live to see me hit a double in my first minor-league game. Didn't share the joy when I became president of a minor-league baseball team and eventually a pro-basketball general manager. And I missed him.

Only now that I am a father myself, do I understand my father. Remembering how I was embarrassed by him, I try to show my support of my own sons at their ball games without embarrassing them. (Actually my problem is more with arguing with the young umpires than with bringing popsicles to the players!)

Fathers and Daughters

In *Passionate Attachments* (Rawson, 1982), Signe Hammer writes about daddy being the first great love of a little girl's life:

If he returns her love in the right way, she will be secure in her femininity forever. If he does not, she can spend the rest of her life looking, desperately, for acceptance and identity.

Indeed, even if Daddy fails us, as he too often does, it is much easier for us to blame ourselves ("I wasn't lovable enough.") than to blame him.

Real intimacy between fathers and daughters may be difficult to achieve. Most men only become intimate with their wives, their sexual partners. And then again, many men don't have a lot of intimacy in them. They are far too passive emotionally, far too conditioned to the patterns of the masculine world, where a kind of emotional neutrality, an emphasis on the surface of things-as-they-are, a focus on process in the real world rather than feelings makes for an easy geniality but not a lot of depth.

In the same book, Dr. John Ross says, "It does seem, for whatever reason, very important for daughters to be adored by their fathers as little children. It validates them. The father mirrors their value."

In "Adjusting to Children," from *How to be Happy Though Married* (Tyndale, 1968), author Tim LaHaye takes up the same topic:

It seems that when a little girl comes to her dad to be loved and is rejected, this rejection makes a lasting scar upon her subconscious mind. If her father never has time for her, never is interested in her little drawings, or does not let her sit on his lap or feel free enough to put her arms around his neck, then in all probability she will develop a protective resistance to her father's rejection to avoid being continually hurt.

Since her first masculine image is her father, she is prone to transfer this image to all men, including her husband. Whatever resentment and hostility she had been fostering in her heart against her father is often transferred to her husband. This faulty, but natural, conditioning process will prepare a girl for a less than ideal marriage and can be avoided by a thoughtful father who recognizes that every little girl needs to be loved by the one man in her life who is most important to her, her dad.

GLOW WORDS

The best gift a father can give to his son is the gift of himself—his time Material things mean little if there is not someone to share them with.

—C. Neil Strait

Fathers and Sons

In their book, *Fathering a Son* (Moody, 1979), Paul Heidebrecht and Jerry Rohrbach point out the necessity of a father fostering independence in his son, and they share two ways to accomplish that:

> First, remember that your example is a huge factor. You have probably learned to value independence because it's a key to success in your own occupation. No doubt you place a high premium on being your own man. Your son will see this, and you are his bridge to the outside world.
>
> Second, you need to balance your wife's influence. She may be overprotective, wanting to shelter your son from potential harm. Make it your job to challenge and test him. Or, if your wife is the one who will encourage your son to try anything, you may have to play the role of protector.

One of the mistakes I am trying to guard against is the very thing that so many fathers do: They work hard to keep their sons from having the problems that made men of their fathers.

The Reverend David C. Fisher, in the April, 1983 issue of *Family Life Today,* wrote his "Thoughts on a Son's 13th Birthday." He tells of how he wept on his son's birthday because he was becoming a teenager, "and I became the father of one."

The child had been sickly at birth but made it through the crucial first twenty-four hours, and then his pastor-father dedicated him, and wept again. Pastor Fisher recalls his son's first day of school. "The look on his face as I left is etched forever in my memory. I cried then, too."

"Usual and unusual events have filled the years: new schools, trips to the hospital for stitches, walks in the woods, spankings, hugs, Little League, moving, good-byes to friends, new friends, vacations, chicken pox, nightmares, insomnia, trikes and bikes and kites, birthday parties, playgrounds, anger, laughter—and I have cried."

Reverend Fisher said he tried, in stumbling words, to put on paper to his son "how much he has meant to me these thirteen years." He says it is more than nostalgia. It is, rather:

An awareness of the awesome gift God has entrusted to me.
The joy of watching a boy become a man.
Understanding that my time of direction is drawing to a close.
Accepting the difficult days which lie just ahead.

And he concludes:

God loves me as a father loves a son. He calls me to love Him as my heavenly Father. His love is tender and purposeful. Just as the life of my son reaches in and grabs my heart, my life touches the heart of almighty God. And like a human father, He reaches out and holds me tight and walks with me through the hard times.

He too has a Son. He watched His Son suffer and die and He shared in the exultation of Easter morning. God understands the pain and joy of parenthood. By His Son's life He calls us to intense and purposeful love. It is thrilling, it hurts, we may shed a tear—but we grow, how we grow!

Charles Francis Adams, the nineteenth century political figure and diplomat, kept a diary. One day he entered: "Went fishing with my son today—a day wasted."

As history would have it, his son Brooks Adams also kept a diary. On that same day, Brooks Adams made this entry: "Went fishing with my father today—the most wonderful day of my life!"

GLOW WORDS

The joy and benefit a child derives from those few precious minutes when he has his parent all to himself far outweighs the temporary inconvenience to the parent of having to delay other duties.

—O. Quentin Hyder
The People You Live With

I often tell the story of a prominent Philadelphia Christian businessman whose wife felt he wasn't spending enough time with his six-year-old daughter. He decided to make up for that failing all at once.

He had his limousine driver take him to her school, where she was picked up and deposited next to him in the backseat. They took off for New York City where he had made reservations for dinner in an expensive French restaurant and had tickets to a Broadway show.

After an exhausting evening, they were driven home. In the morning, the little girl's mother could hardly wait to find out how the evening had gone. "How did you like it?"

The little girl thought a moment. "It was okay, I guess, but I would rather have eaten at McDonald's. And I didn't really understand the show. But the best part was when we were riding home in that great big car and I put my head down on Daddy's lap and fell asleep." Remember our view of quality time versus quantity time?

I also like the story that Fred Smith included in his book, *You and Your Network.* It seems that when his son, Fred, Jr., was married he asked his father to be his best man, since they were best friends.

Smith was deeply honored and sentimental about it and wanted to somehow return the favor.

> I offered to tell him the essence of family management. He replied rather obliquely that he was not going to be an executive but, rather a professor. He also implied that while I had been successful as president of a corporation, I had not enjoyed the same success in managing the home.
>
> Since ours was a close, loving family, I was shocked and asked for more explanation. To which he replied, "You never really understood a father's function, for you tried to be president of the home as you were of the corporation.
>
> "In the company you put production first and relation second. You did the same thing at home. You treated Mother like a vice-president and the rest of us as if we were in the line of organization.

"You would pass orders up and down the line, and if we had grievances, which we had first taken up with our supervisor (Mother), then we could bring them to you for final decision." Sensing he was giving me new information, he smiled and said, "You did the best you could and we love you for it. We operated around you a great deal.

". . . Dad, relation *is* the production in a family. It isn't *what* we accomplish . . . primarily it's that we love each other and secondarily what we do."

For the first time I genuinely understood the essence of family life. Since that time I have tried to think of relations before production, and it has been a very difficult transition. All my reflexes, habits, concepts, were based on a managerial concept rather than a relational one.*

---

* From *You and Your Network* by Fred Smith, copyright © 1984 by Fred Smith; used by permission of Word Books, Publisher, Waco, Texas.

GLOW WORDS

It is never too late to start doing what's right. It may be a difficult process and require a lot of hard work, but it can be done with much prayer and much patience. If there's a will, most dads will find a way.

—Paul Lewis
How Can a Father Win?

John Drescher tells the story of a little fellow, frightened by the lightning and thunder, who called out one dark night, "Daddy, come. I'm scared."

"Oh, son," the father said, "God loves you and He'll take care of you."

"I know God loves me and that He'll take care of me," the small boy replied. "But right now, I want somebody who has skin on."

"If I were starting my family again," Drescher says in his Abingdon book by the same name, "that is what I would want to be—above all else—God's love with skin on. For when the child does not experience God's love, concern, and care from his family, it will be nigh impossible for him to see it or experience it elsewhere in all of life."

I'm one father who knows that it is never too late to start doing what's right by my family. I'm just grateful that I came to my senses while my children were as young as they were—so that not only could they benefit from my commitment to make them a top priority, but so that *I* could as well. And I surely have.

Chapter Ten

Mothering

Blessed are the mothers of the earth, for they have combined the practical and the spiritual into the workable way of human life. They have darned little stockings, mended little dresses, washed little faces, and have pointed little eyes to the stars and little souls to eternal things.

—William L. Stidger

Researchers tell us the single most important factor in the life of the child is his mother. She has more influence on the child than any other person or circumstance. I don't think we're really surprised to hear that, but perhaps once in a while we do need to be reminded of it—and the responsibility it carries.

From the time I was a little girl, when people asked me what I wanted to be when I grew up, I always replied: "Just a plain old mother." And I meant it—because of my own mother. She made the family her top priority and made motherhood seem the most attractive occupation in the world. I loved it that Mom was a "plain old mother," and there was nothing I would rather be. Sometimes I even imagined myself the owner of a huge orphanage where I was everyone's mama and took care of them all.

When I think of carrying out the responsibilities of motherhood, I think of putting into practice those rules of love found in 1 Corinthians 13. What better way to enlarge the circle of love from parents to children. I've written my own paraphrase of this Scripture, which goes like this:

> Love is extraordinarily patient
> Love glories in being kind
> Love is not envious
> Love does not brag or push itself into the limelight
> Love is *never* selfish, but *always* prefers to serve others
> Love is not ostentatious or showy
> Love *never* demands its own way
> Love maintains cool under pressure
> Love does not keep a record of wrongs; in fact, it hardly notices them
> Love is optimistic; it looks at people in the best light
> Love *will not* and *can not* find satisfaction in that which is wrong
> Love covers, shelters, trusts, and protects its loved one in *all* things
> Love searches for what is good and *always* gives the benefit of the doubt
> Love is always filled with hope and optimistic expectations
> Love endures through good times and bad times
> Love never fails, never fades, never falls away
> The greatest thing in all the world is Love

In reading a recent issue of *Family Life Today,* I found that Dianne Lorang had expanded and interpreted that passage in a wonderfully understanding way. I want to share it with you here. You'll see how well it expresses so many of the ideas we've tried to present in this book.

> If I talk to my children about what is right and what is wrong, but have not love, I am like a ringing doorbell or pots banging in the kitchen. And though I know what stages they will go through, and understand their growing pains, and can answer all their questions about life, and believe myself to be a devoted mother, but have not love, I am nothing.
> If I give up the fulfillment of a career to make my children's lives better, and stay up all night sewing costumes or baking

cookies on short notice, but grumble about lack of sleep, I have not love and accomplish nothing.

A loving mother is patient with her children's immaturity and kind even when they are not; a loving mother is not jealous of their youth nor does she hold it over their heads whenever she has sacrificed for them. A loving mother does not push her children into doing things her way. She is not irritable, when the chicken pox have kept her confined with three whining children for two weeks, and does not resent the child who brought the affliction home in the first place.

A loving mother is not relieved when her disagreeable child finally disobeys her directly and she can punish him, but rather rejoices with him when he is being more cooperative. A loving mother bears much of the responsibility for her children; she believes in them; she hopes in each one's individual ability to stand out as a light in a dark world; she endures every backache and heartache to accomplish that.

A loving mother never really dies. As for homebaked bread, it will be consumed and forgotten; as for spotless floors, they will soon gather dust and heelmarks. And as for children, well, right now toys, friends, and food are all-important to them. But when they grow up it will have been how their mother loved them that will determine how they love others. In that way she will live on.

So care, training, and a loving mother reside in a home, these three, but the greatest of these is a loving mother.

Recently, along with other mothers, I was waiting in the car after Bob and Karyn's gymnastics practice when I saw a little girl pick a handful of buttercups from along the side of the road. She ran to her mother, beaming, holding out the bouquet.

The mother brushed them away. "Get those dirty things out of your hands."

As they dropped to the ground, the little girl lowered her chin and fought tears. So did I. If I had it to do over, I would have told her, right in front of her unthinking mother, that she could give me flowers any day.

A week later, I pulled into the same parking lot and the dry, dead flowers were still there. I feared it was a symbolic picture of the relationship between the mother and daughter.

This mother was not practicing loving appreciation for this offering from her child. Rather, she was teaching her daughter that her gift wasn't worthy, and, just possibly, discouraging her from giving in the future. When children grow up it will have been how their mother loved them that will determine how they love others. A mother is always teaching ... something.

Nobody works harder than a mother, unless it's a father pretending to be a mother for twenty-four hours. Anyone other than that who says he or she works harder than a mother is uninformed.

Mothers know this. Others need to think about it. Mothering is not simply doing chores. Mothering is caring, doing, being available, being on call twenty-four hours a day. In fact, even when our children are away from us and in someone else's care, we are still mothering them, perhaps even more than their fathers are fathering them.

GLOW WORDS

Imagine your motherly heart as a large mansion. Each room contains a wealth of information that can lead to better mothering. Behind one door lies the secret of communication, behind another are rare antiques from the storehouse of our memories, and yet another is filled with the sound of laughter. The greatest thing about all these treasures is that they are free. God has given us the keys. Now all we have to do is use them.

—Patricia H. Rushford
What Kids Need Most in a Mom

What's a mother worth?

Experts recently calculated the startling estimate that a mother's annual worth in the employment market would exceed $35,000.

It was calculated that the mother of two preschoolers spends ten hours daily of her working time directly on child care plus being on call for the other two hours of each day and twelve hours each night. Weekly value (regular day care at $4 an hour and on-call care at $3 an hour) was $574.

The weekly housework includes four hours of clothes care, two hours of food shopping, twenty-one hours of food preparation, and five hours of housecleaning. Value of that weekly housework at $3 an hour would be $96.

Then, there are two hours for budgeting and planning and four hours of driving. The weekly worth of those duties is $29.

Total for all above duties is $699 weekly or over $35,000 a year.

These hours, of course, add up to more than twenty-four per day! Truly, a mother's work is never finished.

But who would want to trade it, to miss the unique moments, the priceless comments? Like the time Andrea and I were waiting for the doctor in the examining room. Andrea kept asking, "Mommy, how long will it be?" and I kept answering, "Pretty soon."

Finally Andrea, still getting used to her new language, sighed. "Pretty soon takes long time?"

Karyn's kindergarten class members were told to put their heads down and think about the missionary speaker they had heard. When I put her to bed that night, she said, "When I had my head down, God tapped me on the shoulder and said I could be a missionary."

She was dead serious. And I was teary.

Just before Jim's fifth birthday, Pat was reading to him, when he decided to receive the Lord. He, our quiet one, has given his testimony at Word of Life camp.

For the first several years of your children's lives, busyness permeates your life. First, there's the excitement of learning you're pregnant. Then. . . .

Fear
Wonder
Sickness
Glow
Discomfort
Growing
Fatigue
Movement inside
More wonder
More fear
Prayer
Plans
Names
Preparations
More fear
Waiting
Determination
Examinations
The big day
Pain
Fear
Panic
Agony
Ecstasy
Baby
Name
Phone calls
Wonder
Prayer
Fear
Pictures
Home
The blues
Pain

Recovery
Fatigue
Feeding
Changing
Rocking
Walking
Worrying
Touching

And then, seemingly overnight, you wonder when he learned to walk, to put sentences together, to button his shirt, to tie his shoe, to get the trike's pedals to go the right direction. He feeds himself, wants to choose his own clothes, is on his way to nursery school, then—can it be?—kindergarten.

GLOW WORDS

God is looking for women, for mothers, who trust *Him* to meet their needs. He wants us to pray to Him in our frustrations, and to let Him help us defuse the hurts and angers in our little ones.

—Mevanee Parmer, *Family Life Today*

When your next baby comes along, the routine begins again. This one goes even more quickly. When did she learn all that stuff? How could she be in first grade? I don't remember all the stages? Did she really look that way just two years ago? And why did we shoot so many pictures of the first and so few of the second?

Days are filled with activity. The house is never clean, the dishes never really done, the laundry could be on a conveyor belt. Is he really in third grade already?

You are the busiest person on the face of the earth. Even when you sleep, you are as awake to their sounds as the most sensitive radar screen. The watching, the training, the teaching never stops. During the toddler years it seems you will never stop having to watch his every move, never let him out of your sight. Then he's a gangly sixth grader claiming to hate girls and blushing at the sounds of their names.

You want so much for him, for her, for them. You're their mother. They will grow up, go through puberty, enter a silent adolescence, have their battles with you, yet you will still be their mother.

Your husband, their father, is busy and tired and sometimes exhausted, and you share the task. But he knows. And if he doesn't, down deep you do. The burden is yours. Your day never ends.

They will be collegians, young adults, young marrieds, parents of your grandchildren—and much too strict for grandma's taste—yet you will refer to them not as adults but as your children.

"Offspring" doesn't sound right. "Married son" or "married daughter" is precise, but no, they are your children, no matter their ages. To you they are little ones in adult bodies, still trying their wings. You are proud, you beam as they succeed and prove their abilities. And you remember them at your breast, on the changing table, in the bathtub, in the mud, in the corner, in the doghouse.

You remember Christmases, hurts, tears, prayer, Bible stories, Sunday school, coming to Jesus.

You thrill with their ability to carry on adult conversations. You're amazed at their knowledge, so vast, so beyond you and your education.

Yet they are still your children, your babies. You gave them life. You bore them. You were their life-support system. You were their world. And now they are yours. And they will always be yours.

Because you are a mother. Their mother. And even if they precede you in death, you will always be their mother.